STUDENT WORKBOOK FOR

Groups in Action

Evolution and Challenges,
2nd Edition

Gerald Corey
California State University, Fullerton
Diplomate in Counseling Psychology
American Board of Professional Psychology

Marianne Schneider Corey
Consultant

Robert Haynes
Borderline Productions

Evolution of a Group directed by Thomas Walters
and produced by Robert Haynes

Challenges Facing Group Leaders produced
and directed by Thomas Walters

Lecturette on Theories and Techniques of Group
Counseling produced and directed by Thomas
Walters

BROOKS/COLE
CENGAGE Learning

Australia • Brazil • Japan • Korea • Mexico • Singapore • Spain • United Kingdom • United States

Groups in Action:
Evolution and Challenges, 2nd Edition
Gerald Corey, Marianne Schneider
Corey, Robert Haynes

Executive Editor: Jon-David Hague

Acquisitions Editor: Seth Dobrin

Editorial Assistant: Nicole Bator

Assistant Editor: Naomi Dreyer

Assistant Editor: Suzanna Kincaid

Media Editor: Elizabeth Momb

Content Project Manager:
  Rita Jaramillo

Art Director: Caryl Gorska

Senior Brand Manager:
  Elisabeth Rhoden

Market Development Manager:
  Kara Parsons

Manufacturing Planner: Judy Inouye

Rights Acquisitions Specialist: Thomas
  McDonough

Production and Composition: Cenveo

Text Researcher: Pablo D'Stair

Copy Editor: Kay Mikel

Cover and Text Design: Ingalls Design

Cover Image: Kate Brady

© 2014, 2006 Brooks/Cole, Cengage
  Learning

For product information and technology assistance, contact us at
Cengage Learning Customer & Sales Support, 1-800-354-9706.

For permission to use material from this text or product,
submit all requests online at **www.cengage.com/permissions.**
Further permissions questions can be e-mailed to
permissionrequest@cengage.com.

Library of Congress Control Number: 2012943062

Student Edition:
ISBN-13: 978-1-285-09506-6
ISBN-10: 1-285-09506-5

Brooks/Cole
20 Davis Drive
Belmont, CA 94002-3098
USA

Cengage Learning is a leading provider of customized learning solutions with office locations around the globe, including Singapore, the United Kingdom, Australia, Mexico, Brazil, and Japan. Locate your local office at **www.cengage.com/global.**

Cengage Learning products are represented in Canada by Nelson Education, Ltd.

To learn more about Brooks/Cole, visit **www.cengage.com/brookscole**
Purchase any of our products at your local college store or at our preferred online store **www.CengageBrain.com.**

Printed in the United States of America
15 16 17 18 19 20 21 22 21 20 19 18

CONTENTS

Part III. The Transition Stage   30

Part IV. The Working Stage   41

Part V. The Ending Stage 53

Part VI. Ethical Issues in the Practice of Group Counseling 59

Part VII. Follow-Up Self-Inventory 61

Part VIII. Some Final Thoughts 63

SECOND PROGRAM: Challenges Facing Group Leaders 67

Part I. Overview 68

Part II. Challenges Dealing With Difficult Behaviors in Group 71

THIRD PROGRAM: Lecturette on Theories and
Techniques of Group Counseling 111

Part II. Lecturettes on Theoretical Approaches   114

Introduction

This student workbook is designed to accompany the video *Groups in Action: Evolution and Challenges*. The video and the workbook emphasize the application of concepts and techniques appropriate to the various stages of a group's development and provide an interactive program of self-study for use with group counseling textbooks. The workbook requires that you become an active learner in your study of group process in action.

Key features of the workbook are:

- A group leadership skills checklist
- Process commentaries that address facilitation of the group process and interventions made with individuals
- A summary of member functions, leader functions, and key themes for each of the four group stages
- A strategy for drawing on a variety of techniques
- Questions to consider in understanding group process
- Questions to consider as the leaders assist members doing their work
- Exercises and activities for you to complete individually
- Exercises that can be done in class
- A commentary on group process developments and issues surrounding the work done by individual members
- A list of key points addressed in the video program
- A discussion of why the group leaders intervened as they did at various points in the group
- A discussion of how the group leaders might pursue work with various group members
- A follow-up self-inventory at the end of the program

Groups in Action: Evolution and Challenges consists of three different interactive programs. The first program, *Evolution of a Group*, is a 2-hour educational program designed to bring to life the development of a group at a 3-day residential workshop co-facilitated by Marianne Schneider Corey and Gerald (Jerry) Corey. The group workshop is composed of members who were willing to explore their own issues and concerns. They were neither actors following a script nor were they role-playing the topics. The second program, *Challenges Facing Group Leaders*, is a 90-minute educational program designed to address some of the most problematic situations group counselors often encounter. In this program the Coreys co-facilitated a group composed of members who role-played a variety of scenarios depicting critical issues in a group. The participants did not follow a script but improvised around themes that typically evolve in groups. As participants engaged in role playing, this oftentimes moved into genuine personal involvement and interaction in the group. In short, the participants demonstrate a blend of role-playing and drawing on their experiences from the present and the past, both in their roles as group members and as leaders. The third program, *Lecturette on Theories and Techniques of Group Counseling*, is a 1-hour lecture by Jerry Corey on the main theories of group counseling. This program also describes some techniques associated with the various theoretical frameworks.

NEW TO THIS EDITION

In this Second Edition of *Student Workbook for Groups in Action: Evolution and Challenges*, a number of additions and revisions have been made. The 1-hour *Lecturette on Theories and Techniques of Group Counseling* by Jerry Corey is new to this edition. This video lecture addresses the major therapeutic approaches to group counseling, including psychodynamic, experiential and relationship-oriented, cognitive behavioral, and postmodern approaches. The lecturette concludes with a discussion of how an integrative approach to group counseling draws from a variety of these therapeutic approaches. The student workbook also has a new section to accompany the video lecture, which includes a description of the Main Points and Questions for Reflection for each section of the lecturette.

Responding to student and reviewer input, the workbook Questions for Reflection sections have been streamlined, and a new section, In-Class Exercise: Questions for Small Group Discussion and Reflecting Teams, has been added in eight places to offer relevant activities for in-class discussion regarding the video program.

SYNOPSIS OF THE EDUCATIONAL PROGRAMS

The first program, *Evolution of a Group*, is a compilation of the significant group process and leadership techniques that occurred over a 3-day residential group therapy session. You will see the development of the group process and how the leaders facilitated that process as the group moved through the four stages: initial, transition, working, and ending.

In the initial stage, the focus is on building trust and focusing on the here and now. The leaders set the stage by exploring ground rules for the group operation and assisting members in developing their goals.

In the transition stage, identifying and challenging member fears, hesitations, and resistance are the main topics. The level of trust is deepening, and members begin reluctantly to talk about personal material.

The working stage is characterized by a high level of trust, clearer goals, and members exploring feelings, ideas, and beliefs. The leaders help members explore their issues by focusing on the here and now so that members are not just "talking about" their issues but are actually experiencing them. Group cohesiveness is high, and members interact with each other with less reliance on the leaders.

In the ending stage, group members review what they have learned, discuss how they will put their learning into action, and prepare for ending the group.

Throughout the program we (Marianne and Jerry Corey) colead and facilitate the group process using a variety of group techniques from various group treatment approaches. We strive to facilitate mutual trust and to support members, challenging them when needed, and at times, using humor therapeutically. It is the combination of viewing both the implementation of group leadership techniques and the movement of the group through the four stages of group process that makes this a unique video training program.

The second program, *Challenges Facing Group Leaders*, consists of improvisational enactments of problematic scenarios and critical incidents in a group. The Coreys encouraged the participants of this second program to be themselves as much as possible, even though they were at times enacting different roles. Some of the scenarios enacted include working with members who do not want to be a part of the group; dealing with a group when it is making little progress; addressing conflict; dealing with silence; exploring a member's reactions to being left with unresolved feelings about a prior group session; working with members who are uncomfortable expressing emotions; addressing a member's concern over feeling pressured to talk; managing a member who assumes a role of assistant leader; dealing with trust issues and concerns about confidentiality; working with a quiet member; and the challenges in dealing with a range of difficult behaviors in groups.

A significant part of this second program demonstrates ways that diversity influences group process. A few of the issues addressed pertaining to diversity include experiencing identity concerns; feeling different from others; dealing with stereotypes; speaking in one's primary language; looking to leaders for answers; and looking at the ways in which people are both the same and different.

The second program is intended to teach ways of understanding and effectively working with a range of challenging situations that group counselors frequently encounter, especially during the early stages of a group. Key points illustrated in the *Challenges Facing Group Leaders* program include the following:

- Leaders cannot afford to bypass developments in group process.
- Group work is slow and tedious at times and demands patience on the leader's part.
- Group facilitators have the responsibility of creating safety within a group.
- A group leader has the task of encouraging members to deal with issues that could impede their willingness to make themselves vulnerable and take risks in a group.
- The earlier phases of a group are critical in terms of laying a solid foundation for work at the later stages.

- Group counselors need to be prepared to continuously deal with issues that may emerge at a later time in a group.
- Work takes place at all stages of group, not just during the beginning stages.
- How effectively a leader deals with challenges from group members at an early stage determines how effective the group will eventually become.
- Diversity is a reality that cannot be overlooked in a group. The group setting offers participants a valuable opportunity to explore concerns that they often face outside of the group.

The third program, *Theories and Techniques of Group Counseling*, consists of a lecture featuring four general theories that are briefly described in a new chapter in *Groups: Process and Practice* (M. Corey, G. Corey, & C. Corey, 2014). The general theoretical orientations covered in the lecture include psychodynamic approaches, experiential and relationship-oriented therapies, cognitive behavioral therapies, and postmodern approaches.

LEARNING OBJECTIVES FOR GROUPS IN ACTION: EVOLUTION AND CHALLENGES

After viewing the video and completing the student workbook for the first program, *Evolution of a Group*, you will be better able to do the following:

1. Identify the major characteristics of each of the stages of a group
2. Apply certain techniques in opening and closing a group session
3. Discuss the importance of focusing on here-and-now interactions
4. Understand how past experiences can be worked with in the present
5. Discuss the value of self-awareness in knowing your values and how they affect you as a group counselor
6. Identify the major tasks of group leadership at each stage of a group
7. Identify the major functions and roles of coleaders
8. Identify the roles and expectations of group members at the various stages of a group
9. Discuss how group leaders can effectively work with issues of cultural diversity
10. Discuss the importance of building a climate of trust in a group setting
11. Discuss ways to formulate an agenda for a group session
12. Apply specific skills that help members formulate personal goals in a group

After viewing the video and completing the student workbook for the second program, *Challenges Facing Group Leaders*, you will be better able to do the following:

13. Identify the major problem situations facing group leaders
14. Discuss the major techniques used by the Coreys in dealing with challenging group situations
15. Reframe resistance in more useful ways
16. Appreciate the importance of establishing a foundation during the early phase of a group that will allow for productive interchanges as a group evolves
17. Develop some objectivity in dealing with a range of difficult behaviors that are often exhibited by group members
18. Understand ways to most effectively work with transference and countertransference reactions
19. Understand the importance of being aware of your own fears and concerns in working with challenging situations
20. Discuss the role of respect and trust in working with groups
21. Understand the importance of trust in the group process and not be afraid of conflict and not have pat responses for the variety of problem situations that might arise
22. Discuss the importance of identifying differences and commonalities among the group members
23. Understand that the group leader does not need to know everything about every culture
24. Appreciate the ways in which many forms of diversity can add richness to a group experience

After viewing the video and completing the student workbook for the third program, *Theories and Techniques of Group Counseling*, you will be better able to do the following:

25. Appreciate the value of identifying a theoretical framework for the practice of group work
26. See the link between theory and techniques in group work
27. Explain the importance of understanding transference and countertransference
28. Understand how the past influences a group member's present experience
29. Grasp ways that psychodynamic approaches can be applied to a wide range of groups
30. Identify specific concepts from the relationship-oriented approaches to various kinds of groups
31. Identify concepts from the cognitive behavioral approaches that have relevance for group practice
32. Understand how the postmodern approaches offer a new perspective for group practitioners

RESOURCE TEXTBOOKS

This student workbook is designed to provide a self-study guide for you as you view the video. It is also designed as a supplement to several of the Coreys' textbooks in group counseling, and it can be used as a combined package of video, workbook, and textbook. The video and workbook also can be effectively coupled with other standard group counseling textbooks.

We frequently refer to the following three textbooks—all published by Brooks-Cole, Cengage Learning—as they are ideal companions to your self-study program and this workbook:

- *Groups: Process and Practice* (9th Edition, 2014) (coauthored by Marianne Schneider Corey, Gerald Corey, and Cindy Corey)
- *Group Techniques* (3rd Edition, 2004) (coauthored by Gerald Corey, Marianne Schneider Corey, Patrick Callanan, and J. Michael Russell)
- *Theory and Practice of Group Counseling* (8th Edition, 2012) and *Student Manual for Theory and Practice of Group Counseling* (by Gerald Corey)

WELCOME TO THE SELF-STUDY PROGRAM

We hope you view the video with an openness to learning about how group process works—and with a willingness to examine your own beliefs as a group leader. This program can provide the experiential piece that helps you more concretely understand the nature of group process, and it can be a catalyst that prompts your self-exploration. Your ability to function effectively as a group leader has a great deal to do with the degree to which you possess self-awareness and are willing to draw on your personal resources in facilitating others in understanding themselves. The art of group leadership is far more than a technical endeavor; it involves your capacity to use your intuition and human responses. To be sure, effective group leaders need a theoretical grasp of group process along with the knowledge and skill base to make effective interventions in a group. Competent group leaders possess self-understanding, knowledge of the dynamics of behavior and group process, and technical skills in group facilitation.

In teaching courses in group counseling or when training group leaders, we often ask students to participate in a group session and work with some of their real concerns. We find that this experiential learning contributes to a deeper understanding and appreciation of group work in actual practice. Through their own participation in a group experience, they are able to recognize their countertransference and unfinished business that could impede their therapeutic work with clients. It seems much more meaningful for students to talk about matters such as trust building, confrontation, providing feedback, working with resistance, and working in the here and now as they actually experience each of these in a group situation—rather than relying solely on learning about group process from readings and lectures. We hope the combination of this video, workbook, and group counseling textbook provides you with a more realistic picture of the power inherent in a cohesive group.

HOW TO MAKE BEST USE OF THE VIDEO AND WORKBOOK

This video is not designed to be a stand-alone program. It is essential that the video be utilized in conjunction with the student workbook in the context of a course or workshop along with a textbook on groups. For the first program (*Evolution of a Group*), the original 20 hours of the actual group process was edited down to less than 2 hours. The student workbook provides a context for those portions of the group not seen in the video. The second program (*Challenges Facing Group Leaders*) has been edited from a 2-day group to a 90-minute video. With both programs, the workbook gives a basis for understanding the action that is taking place and provides a rationale for the coleaders' interventions. The commentaries and reflections provided by the Coreys in the workbook assist viewers in grasping the key ideas of both programs.

A Guide for Reviewing the Program: *Evolution of a Group*

The purpose of the first video program, *Evolution of a Group*, is to provide you with an opportunity to observe how a real group in action evolves from the beginning to the end. The aim of the video is to raise questions and issues, and to help you understand the art of facilitating a group. We do this by demonstrating how the various stages of a group, which we describe in our group texts, are played out within the group.

This video is a major visual tool that presents a demonstration of the evolution of a group. Although the video provides less than 2 hours of condensed material, the workbook supplies some process commentary on material that you may not see in the video. We hope you will use the workbook as your "interpreter" of the group process. In the workbook we provide a rationale for the interventions we have made, discuss where an individual's work moved beyond what is shown in the video, and involve you in what you are viewing by providing questions for your response.

You may want to watch the entire video without interruption once to get a sense of the general unfolding of the group. Then watch the video, stopping at each pause point, identified by an icon with the stage and number that corresponds to sections in the workbook. For each segment of work, or for each main interaction within the group, the workbook asks a series of questions pertaining to the situation you are seeing.

As you watch the video, imagine what it would be like if you were a group member, then put yourself into the situation as a group leader. As you study the video from the group leader's perspective, think of the leadership skills needed to effectively intervene, and reflect on the way you might approach therapeutic work with individual members.

Icons indicating pause points occur throughout the video and refer you to the workbook to help you assess and clarify your thinking, both as a member and as a leader. Ask yourself the following questions after every segment of work within a stage of the group:

1. What do you imagine it would be like to be the group member in this particular situation? If you were the member, how much trust would you feel?
2. What issues come up for you as you watch a particular member work or observe interactions between members?
3. What reactions do you have to how the group leaders worked with each group member?
4. What are you learning about the use of group leadership skills and techniques from viewing a particular interaction?
5. What is the degree of trust you sense in the group?
6. How are the coleaders working together?
7. What are you learning about applying group process concepts to an actual group from viewing specific segments of work?
8. How can you apply what you are viewing to working with different kinds of groups?

We have found that people who viewed this group were emotionally affected because observing the work of the members triggered personal issues. For instance, the production crew who participated in making this video were all very much moved by what they saw and heard during the weekend group. Even though they were professionals with a job to do, they also found themselves drawn into the genuine interactions that unfolded. We suspect that many of you will identify with some of the members of this group, as the themes explored in this group represent universal human struggles.

Group leaders bring to their professional work their life experiences and their personal characteristics. If you plan to lead groups, it is essential that you are aware of any unresolved personal conflicts—and that you demonstrate a willingness to address these conflicts. We believe you will be able to facilitate a member's work only to the degree that you have been willing to engage in your own journey into yourself. If you have led an unexamined life, it is not likely that you will have the resources to inspire others to challenge themselves to take the risks necessary for growth. For a more complete discussion of the personal characteristics of an effective group leader, refer to the discussion in *Groups: Process and Practice* (Chapter 2), *Group Techniques* (Chapter 1), and *Theory and Practice of Group Counseling* (Chapter 2).

One way of getting more from the video for your own personal growth is to discuss your reactions with others. You can do this by getting a small study group together for the purpose of exchanging ideas or by talking to another person in your class. Different individuals will bring different perspectives to what is being seen. Furthermore, students and practitioners observing this group in action will most likely have many different ideas about ways to proceed with individual members and how to deal with interactions within the group. We do not want to communicate the idea that there is only one right intervention for each problem situation. In deciding how to make interventions in a group, leaders are influenced by what draws their interest, their theoretical orientation, their level of experience, and a host of other factors. Being in a small group can stimulate discussion of the many ways of pursuing therapeutic work in a group.

Throughout the workbook you will encounter Questions for Discussion and Reflection. Most of these questions have no right or wrong answer; they are designed to get you to explore your own thoughts about and reactions to the group interactions and group leadership techniques. We hope you will use these opportunities for self-reflection and self-learning on your journey to becoming an effective group leader.

ABOUT THE PARTICIPANTS

The First Program: *Evolution of a Group*

We would like to thank the group members for participating in the development of the first educational video program, *Evolution of a Group*. We admire the participants for their courage to be themselves and for their willingness to explore real concerns and issues. Their work in this project provided an opportunity for viewers to see a real group in action rather than one that was scripted or role-played. The additional benefit of the group members' work is that many viewers may be touched in a way that serves as a catalyst to do their own work as well. The participants in this program were all graduates of an undergraduate program in human services and most of them were enrolled in graduate studies in counseling or social work, or had completed their advanced degrees. Some of them work in mental health agency settings as counselors.

Thanks to the group members who participated in *Evolution of a Group*:

Andrew	Jacqueline
Casey	James
Darren	Jyl
Jackie	SusAnne

The Second Program: *Challenges Facing Group Leaders*

Our appreciation also goes to those who participated in the second program, *Challenges Facing Group Leaders*. They are to be commended for drawing upon their own experiences as group members and also as facilitators of their groups. They managed to be themselves in many respects while at the same time getting involved in role enactments to illustrate ways to deal with problematic situations in groups. The participants in this program were all graduates from an undergraduate human services program. Some of them have master's degrees in social work or counseling, and others are pursuing graduate degrees in one of the helping professions. All of them have been members in several groups as a part of their undergraduate human services program, and all of them have facilitated or are currently leading groups with various populations.

Thanks to the group members who participated in *Challenges Facing Group Leaders*:

Galo Arboleda	Joel Cisneros
Nicole Nanchy	Nadine Newhouse Session
Maria Ostheimer	George Spraggings
Vivian Vu	Toni Wallace

Group Leadership Skills: A Checklist

As you watch the video, think about how you would apply the various leadership skills to specific pieces of work you observe. At many of the icons, you can explore the skills you would need to intervene effectively. Try to identify specific group leadership skills that are being demonstrated by the coleaders, and use the following questions to reflect on your strengths and weaknesses as a group leader:

1. Active listening
    a. How well are you able to listen to members?
    b. Are you sensitive to nonverbal messages?
    c. What can get in your way of listening to others?

2. Reflecting
    a. Are you able to reflect without sounding rehearsed?
    b. Are you able to reflect both content and feelings accurately?
    c. Do your reflections help members explore more fully what they are feeling?

3. Clarifying
    a. Does your clarification help clients sort out their feelings?
    b. Do members get a clearer sense of what they are thinking and feeling through your clarifications?
    c. Do your clarifications typically lead to increased member self-exploration?

4. Summarizing
    a. Are you able to identify common themes in a session?
    b. Can you help give direction through your summary remarks?
    c. Are you able to give an accurate summary, especially at the end of a session?

5. Facilitating
    a. Are you able to assist members in identifying and expressing whatever they are experiencing in the present?
    b. Do you foster interaction among the members?
    c. Are your interventions designed to increase the level of member responsibility for what happens in the group?

6. Empathizing
    a. Do your life experiences provide a basis for genuinely understanding the struggles of your members?
    b. Can you express your empathy to members so that they feel understood by you?
    c. Are you able to identify with others without getting overly involved and lost in their pain?

7. Interpreting
    a. Do you present your interpretations in such a manner that members are encouraged to think about what you say?
    b. How often are your interpretations appropriate and well timed?
    c. To what degree do you encourage members to make their own interpretations?

8. Questioning
    a. Do you use open or closed questions more frequently?
    b. What impact do your questions have on members?
    c. Do you ask "how" questions or "why" questions?

9. Linking
    a. Do your interventions foster member-to-member interactions or leader-to-member interactions?
    b. Do you value promoting an interactional focus in a group?
    c. How do you pay attention to cues that indicate common concerns?

10. Confronting
    a. To what degree do your confrontations invite people to look at themselves?
    b. What kind of modeling do you provide for effective confrontation?
    c. Are your confrontations related to specific behavior rather than being global and judgmental?

11. Supporting
    a. To what degree do you provide positive reinforcement to members?
    b. Do you know when it is appropriate to offer support and when it is wise not to give support?
    c. Does your support result in members continuing a process of self-exploration, or does it lead to closure of an issue?

12. Blocking
    a. Are you aware of what behaviors to block in a group?
    b. Are you able to intervene effectively when a member is engaging in counterproductive behavior?
    c. Do you block firmly yet sensitively?

13. Diagnosing
    a. Can you make an assessment without labeling a person?
    b. Are you able to assess what a group needs at a given time?
    c. Do you know when a particular group might be counterproductive for an individual?

14. Reality testing
    a. Do you help members to explore alternatives?
    b. Do you encourage members to test the reality base of their plans?
    c. To what degree do you teach members to apply what they learn in the group to their everyday lives?

15. Evaluating
    a. Do you teach members to continuously assess their level of participation in a group?
    b. Do you employ systematic means of evaluating a group?
    c. Do you spend some time openly discussing the progress of a group with the members?

16. Terminating
    a. Are you able to assist members in consolidating what they have learned in a group?
    b. Do you structure a group so that members are encouraged to transfer in-group learning to situations outside of the group?
    c. Do you encourage members to continue working after the ending of a group?

FIRST PROGRAM:

Evolution of a Group

Part I: Forming a Group

About Forming This Group. The group shown in this 2-hour video is a closed, time-limited intensive group that met for about 20 working hours. In this workbook, we base our teaching points both on what you will see in the video and, in some instances, on segments that were edited from the video due to time constraints. The workbook fills in some of the gaps, and it provides a way for us to make some additional teaching points. We describe how a particular situation developed, how we continued working with members, and how they arrived at certain insights.

The group consisted of eight members (five women and three men) and two coleaders. Although this group met as a residential group over 3 consecutive days for filming, we want to emphasize that the process we describe (in both the video and in this workbook) does not differ a great deal from the process of a group that meets weekly. Certainly, the techniques we demonstrate could be used in groups that meet weekly, and many of the concerns the members raised are no different from personal issues typically explored in many therapy groups. Throughout this workbook, we ask how you might transfer what you are seeing to the specific type of group or particular population with which you may work.

All the participants in this group had some prior group experience. None were current students of ours, but all had participated in personal-growth groups we coled at various times. Few of the participants knew each other prior to agreeing to participate in this video. Most of them are in the helping professions and have at least a bachelor's degree in human services. One was in a doctoral program in counseling. Two participants have master's degrees in counseling, two were currently enrolled in master's degree programs in counseling, and several soon went on for graduate study in the helping professions.

Pregroup Meeting. It is ideal to arrange for a pregroup meeting after members have been screened and selected. This meeting is an orientation session where we provide further information regarding the group to help the members consider whether this group is suitable for them. There were many special issues for these group members to consider regarding the filming and educational use of the material such as informed consent, confidentiality, and revealing sensitive personal information.

At the pregroup meeting, potential members had the opportunity to get acquainted with one another and to determine whether they wanted to participate in this type of special group experience. Of course, all the participants knew in advance that the purpose of this workshop was to produce an educational program. We discussed at length the special circumstances associated with participating in a group that is being filmed. We wanted members to be themselves by sharing their real concerns, yet we emphasized that they would decide what specific personal subjects they would be willing to introduce. We reassured them that they had control over what would or would not be included in the final program. Throughout the weekend, they had opportunities to tell us if they wanted to omit any portion of their actual work. The members' veto power was repeated at the pregroup meeting, during the weekend sessions, and after members returned home. We wanted them to have an opportunity to reflect on the work they did after the intensity of the weekend had subsided and to communicate any afterthoughts or reservations regarding the inclusion of some aspect of their participation in the final version of the video.

In the video you will first see the initial stage of the group, which is a period of getting acquainted, establishing group norms and ground rules, and beginning to develop a sense of trust. We assist group members in developing goals for their group work and identifying what might get in the way of accomplishing these goals. We directly address their hopes and expectations and also their fears and anxieties about the group, and we focus members on the here and now.

Importance of Preliminary Preparation. Many groups that get stuck at some point do so because the foundations were poorly laid at the outset. What is labeled as "resistance" on the part of group members is often the result of the leader's failure to provide members with adequate orientation. Preparation can begin at the individual screening and can be continued during the initial session.

Although building pregroup preparation into the design of a group takes considerable effort, careful planning and preparation can avoid many potential barriers to a group's progress.[1]

SUMMARY OF ISSUES IN FORMING A GROUP

The video does not show the selection process, the steps that were taken in getting ready for the video, the pregroup meeting that took place 7 weeks before the filming, or other important procedures leading to the formation of this group. This summary of key issues pertaining to member functions and leader functions will give you a more complete picture of what led up to the actual first meeting that you see in the video.

Member Functions. Before joining a group, individuals need to have the knowledge necessary to make an informed decision concerning their participation. Members should be active in the process of deciding whether a group is right for them. Following are some issues that pertain to the role of members at the formation stage:

- Members should know all the specifics about a group that might have an impact on them.
- Members can profit by preparing themselves for the upcoming group by thinking about what they want from the experience and identifying personal themes that will guide their work in a group.

Leader Functions. The main tasks of group leaders during the formation of a group include the following:

- Identifying general goals and specific purposes of the group
- Developing a clearly written proposal for the formation of a group
- Providing adequate information to prospective participants so they can make an informed decision
- Conducting interviews for screening and orientation purposes
- Selecting members, and attending to members who are not selected
- Organizing the practical details necessary to launch a successful group
- Preparing psychologically for leadership tasks and meeting with coleaders (if appropriate)
- Arranging for a preliminary group session to get acquainted, present ground rules, and prepare the members for a successful group experience
- Making provisions for informed consent and exploring with participants the potential risks involved in a group experience
- Discussing the importance of confidentiality, including the limitations of confidentiality in groups

QUESTIONS FOR DISCUSSION AND REFLECTION

1. In setting up a group, what are some of the major factors you would want to consider?
2. How would you go about recruiting, screening, and selecting members for one of your groups?
3. What do you think you need to do as a group leader to assist members in giving informed consent?
4. What kind of preparation would you want to provide to members of your groups? How might you orient them to the group experience?

---

[1] For a more detailed discussion of issues pertaining to forming a group, see *Groups: Process and Practice* (Chapter 5). For a discussion of getting groups established and conducting a preliminary group session, see *Group Techniques* (Chapter 3). For issues pertaining to forming a group, see *Theory and Practice of Group Counseling* (Chapter 4, textbook and student manual).

Part II: The Initial Stage

Directions: Complete this brief self-inventory before viewing the initial stage of the group. The purpose of the self-inventory is to help you identify and clarify your attitudes and beliefs about a variety of group process concepts, techniques, and issues in group leadership. The statements on the inventory are not simply right or wrong, true or false. The point is to get you in an active frame of mind as you watch and reflect on the video and as you complete the workbook activities. Decide the degree to which you agree or disagree with these statements. Then, after viewing this segment, look over your responses to see whether you want to modify them in any way. These self-inventories will help you express your views and will prepare you to actively read and think about the ideas you'll encounter in this self-study program.

Using the following code, write next to each statement the number of the response that most closely reflects your viewpoint:

5 = I *strongly agree* with this statement.
4 = I *agree*, in most respects, with this statement.
3 = I am *undecided* in my opinion about this statement.
2 = I *disagree*, in most respects, with this statement.
1 = I *strongly disagree* with this statement.

_____ 1. I think it is absolutely necessary to conduct a careful screening process for the groups I will lead.

_____ 2. If at all possible, I would arrange for a pregroup meeting for orientation purposes.

_____ 3. In a well-conducted group, there are really no psychological risks for the group participants.

_____ 4. As a group leader, it is my job to establish ground rules for the participants.

_____ 5. Confidentiality is one of the most basic issues that needs to be addressed early in the course of a group.

_____ 6. A major function of leaders during the initial stage is to assist members in formulating concrete and personal goals.

_____ 7. As a way of creating an accepting climate, I'd engage in a fair degree of self-disclosure.

_____ 8. In general, there are more advantages than disadvantages to using a coleadership model in a group.

The First Session. As you can see in the video, at the outset we ask the members to silently look around the room. Members typically make assumptions about others in the group, and we hope they will eventually check out these assumptions to determine their validity. At this point, they are not asked to verbalize their reactions, but simply to note them. The purpose of asking people to look around the room and silently reflect is so that they can center themselves and get a sense of what they are thinking and feeling at the moment, especially their early reactions toward others. This will be useful material upon which we will draw at later sessions. At this early phase, we make a concerted effort to teach participants how to pay attention to their own reactions and behavior in the context of what is occurring in the session.

We also make a bridge from the first time we met as a group, at the pregroup meeting. We ask them to say their names, mention any thoughts they have had since the pregroup meeting, and describe what it is like for them to come to this meeting. After they give their name, they are asked to repeat the names of all those who have spoken before them. By doing this, everyone learns the names of group members and everyone participates verbally. An indirect outcome is that members typically speak up quickly because they are concerned about remembering all the names.

The specific leadership skills that are especially important at this first session of the weekend group are active listening, reflecting, clarifying, facilitating, and supporting. As you watch each segment of action on the video, refer to the group leadership skills listed earlier in this workbook. Identify the skills you think are most important at this time, and reflect on the degree to which you are able to apply each skill. Consider which skills represent your areas of strength and which skills need improvement.[2]

QUESTIONS FOR DISCUSSION AND REFLECTION

At the various pause points in the video, we have supplied a process commentary explaining the reasons for our interventions or discussing member interactions or work. We raise questions for you to consider, both as a group leader and as a group member. We suggest that you think about a specific type of group and a specific age population and apply the questions to a group you expect to lead. What modifications might you make? What cultural factors will you take into consideration? What skills might you apply to a particular situation? How would you implement the specific techniques we identify?

Taking the time to reflect on these questions and writing down your responses will assist you in learning practical applications. In deciding what to write as a leader response to different situations, we hope that you give yourself latitude by experimenting with a range of responses. We find that students freeze up when they are overly concerned about making mistakes and when they are too focused on saying and doing the "right" thing. The purpose of this workbook is to give you practice in clarifying your thinking and refining your responses. Rather than burden yourself with giving "right" or "wrong" responses, let yourself give more immediate responses to the situations you observe in the group. As you review what you've written, you can always rethink your reasoning for an intervention.

In addition to thinking about these questions from the leader's perspective, imagine yourself as a member of this group and respond from that vantage point. It will be useful to compare your responses with fellow students in a small group or in a class.

1. What kind of group are you most interested in designing and leading? Name some specific issues to address in starting this group.

_____

_____

_____

2. If you were to arrange a pregroup meeting for a group you are forming, what would you most want to accomplish at this meeting? What would you most want to know?

_____

_____

_____

3. If you were a member in this group, what do you imagine it would be like for you? What would be your concerns and expectations?

_____

_____

_____

4. What purpose do you see in asking members to spend a few minutes in silence as they look around the room? What would you ask members to do or say after this, if anything?

_____

_____

_____

_____

[2] For a more detailed discussion of techniques for getting acquainted, focusing members, and teaching them how to pay attention to the group process, see *Group Techniques* (Chapter 4). For a discussion of the survey of group leadership skills, see *Groups: Process and Practice* (Chapter 2); see also *Theory and Practice of Group Counseling* (Chapter 2, textbook and student manual).

5. What information would you want to know prior to making a commitment to being a member in a group?

_____

_____

_____

INTRODUCING THE GROUP MEMBERS

Let us introduce you to the group members with a brief sketch of each in terms of what they say about themselves early in the group and what they might want to explore during the weekend:

- Jacqueline (late 40s) sometimes does not feel a part of various groups in which she is involved. She refers to herself as an African American woman who at times finds it difficult to relate to others and states that she often feels "marginalized." One of her goals is to explore ways in which she seeks approval from others.

- SusAnne (age 27), a Latina, would like to explore relationships in her life. She wants to explore the price she is paying for staying safe and not taking the risks of pursuing the relationships she wants.

- Jyl (age 39), a Euro-American, is willing to deal with struggles pertaining to perfectionism, dealing with losses, and career aspirations. Jyl experiences difficulty in asking others for what she wants, or in letting others care for her.

- James (age 35) describes himself as an educated Chicano who feels that he has to "prove himself." Because of his cultural background, he often feels oppressed in certain situations.

- Andrew (age 35), a Euro-American, is struggling with deciding how close he wants to get to people, especially women. Having gone through a painful divorce, he is very protective of letting himself get involved in an intimate relationship again.

- Darren (age 27), of Hispanic background, sometimes worries about how he expresses himself and is concerned about the impression he makes. He sometimes feels too young, and it is difficult for him to fit in with a group. He realizes that he wants to feel a sense of belonging.

- Casey (age 23) refers to herself as a Vietnamese American. She struggles with messages she received as a child that now get in her way. She would like to challenge her fears of feeling judged that hold her back at times.

- Jackie (age 43), a Euro-American, puts a lot of pressure on herself to be perfect, to get everyone to like her, and to keep everyone happy. She sometimes feels that she is not good enough, no matter what she accomplishes.

Setting Goals. One of the main tasks during the initial stage is for the leader to assist members in identifying clear and specific goals that will influence their participation. For group sessions to have direction, it is essential that members clarify what they want from a group. This process of setting goals is important both at the beginning of a new group and at the start of each group meeting. Too often members come up with fuzzy and global goals; in this case, the leader's task is to help members translate vague goals into clear and workable goals. Furthermore, it is crucial that members establish goals that have personal meaning for them, as opposed to setting goals that others think are important for them to pursue. Members who are working on their own goals are more motivated than those who are talking about a particular behavior they think they *should* change.[3]

1. Refer to the list of group leadership skills. What skills do you deem most important in assisting members to formulate clear personal goals?

_____

_____

_____

---

[3] For a more detailed discussion of ways to identify and clarify group member goals, see *Groups: Process and Practice* (Chapter 6). See also *Group Techniques* (Chapter 3) and *Theory and Practice of Group Counseling* (Chapter 4, textbook and student manual).

2. If members state goals in vague terms, what might you say to assist them in establishing concrete goals?

_____

_____

_____

Note: The video segment labeled "[icon] 1 Initial Stage" corresponds to the workbook "Section 1" ("View Video Section 1: Early Developments and Interactions") and so on throughout this program.

VIEW THE BEGINNING OF THE VIDEO AND STOP AT SECTION 1

Early Developments and Interactions
VIEW VIDEO SECTION 1: EARLY DEVELOPMENTS AND INTERACTIONS

From the outset we ask members to briefly report some things they've been thinking about since the pregroup meeting and what they are aware of at this moment as they are convening for this weekend group. James says he often feels like an outsider in his life. As we listen to James, our interest is in finding out how James perceives himself in this group. We ask him, "Do you feel like an outsider in here?" We hope he will verbalize what it is like to be an outsider both in and out of group.

Jacqueline reports that she feels stupid and thinks that she rambles and makes no sense. It is important to find out what feeling stupid and being inarticulate mean to her. We do not assume that we know what she means by rambling. Our interest is in finding out if and how this is problematic for her. We have a hunch that she has a critical judge within her; however, we do not pursue this at this time. Instead, we ask her to mention a few ways that feeling stupid gets in the way of what she wants.

Andrew acknowledges that, like James, he feels like an outsider. When Marianne inquires whether he feels like an outsider with everyone in this group and whether there are some with whom he can make a connection, he tells us that he finds it is easier to trust the men in the group. The inquiry is aimed at getting Andrew to note that he does not feel equally distant from everyone. Again, we do not assume that we know what being an outsider means to Andrew or James, nor do we know what feeling stupid is like for Jacqueline, so we ask all three of them to note and verbalize when they become aware of these feelings.

As you look at this segment of action in the video, consider the following questions and your response to them.

1. What group leadership skills are especially important in the initial stage?

_____

_____

2. What purpose do you see in asking members to state verbally what they have been thinking or feeling before a session?

_____

_____

3. James says, "I feel like an outsider." How might you work with his statement?

_____

_____

4. Jacqueline says, "I feel stupid when I ramble." How would you deal with her statement in the first session?

_____

_____

Some Teaching About Group

VIEW VIDEO SECTION 2: SOME TEACHING ABOUT GROUP

We know that confidentiality is essential if members are to feel a sense of safety in a group, and it is basic for them to be willing to engage in risk-taking. Even if nobody raises this issue, we raise the topic and caution members about how confidentiality can be broken. We provide guidelines for maintaining the confidential nature of the exchanges. Specifically, we emphasize how easy it might be to break confidentiality without intending to do so. We ask members to refrain from talking about what others are doing in the group. We emphasize to members that it is their responsibility to continually make the room safe by addressing their concerns regarding how their disclosures will be treated. If they do not feel trust because they are afraid that others will talk outside the group, this doubt will certainly hamper their ability to fully participate.

We also mention to members that it does not make sense to open up too quickly without a foundation of trust. As is evident in the video, the way to create trust is to get members to verbalize their fears, concerns, and here-and-now reactions during the early sessions. We emphasize that it is up to each member to decide what to talk about and how far to pursue a topic. During the early phase of a group, we are not likely to make interventions that lead to in-depth exploration of what members are saying. Rather than focusing immediately on the first member who speaks, we make sure that everybody has a chance to briefly introduce him- or herself.[4]

1. You are meeting your group for the first session. What would you most want to tell them about confidentiality?

_____

_____

_____

2. What would you do to facilitate the development of trust at the first meeting of a group?

_____

_____

3. Imagine yourself as a member at the first meeting. What fears would you have about participating? What would help you feel more trusting?

_____

_____

The Dyad Exercise

VIEW VIDEO SECTION 3: THE DYAD EXERCISE

Marianne gives instructions to members about how to make the best use of the group, and then introduces a dyad exercise. Working in pairs facilitates member interaction because talking to one

---

[4] For a discussion of techniques for creating trust, see _Group Techniques_ (Chapter 4). For a discussion of specific attitudes and actions leading to trust, see _Groups: Process and Practice_ (Chapter 6). For a discussion of factors to consider during the early phases of groups, see _Theory and Practice of Group Counseling_ (Chapter 4, textbook and student manual).

person seems less threatening than addressing the entire group. We ask members to say a few things to their partners that they have been thinking about since we first met at the pregroup meeting. Specifically, we suggest they talk about any fears or expectations they have about this group, and anything they hope to explore in the group. We typically have them talk for about 10 minutes to a partner and give them a chance to participate in a couple of dyads. After the dyads, we ask members to take turns verbalizing to the entire group a few of the points they shared with their partner(s) in this exercise. Again, our aim is to hear from everyone, to clarify what they are saying, and to help them become more specific about their goals for the group. We avoid interventions that would facilitate deeper exploration for any of the members because we want ample time for all members to at least identify their concerns. Although it may be tempting to stay with any one member for a great deal of time to work on what he or she initially brings up, we do not do so because it would be at the expense of including others. If all participants speak early on, it provides everyone with a better sense of each other. They usually discover some commonalities enabling them to identify with one another, which leads to a climate of trust.[5]

1. How might you modify the dyad exercise when you think about a particular group that you expect to be leading? What issues might arise when using the dyad exercise for your group?

_____

_____

_____

2. What ideas do you have about ways to begin a first group session? How would you promote interaction?

_____

_____

_____

OUR GOALS AND EXPECTATIONS FOR THE BEGINNING OF A GROUP

In this section, we describe some specific norms we are actively attempting to shape during the first few group sessions and some relevant examples from the video. We make the assumption that participants will get the most from a group experience if they are taught how to best involve themselves in active ways during the sessions.

Full Participation

We expect everybody to become a participating member. If members do not bring themselves in spontaneously, we continue to encourage them to speak. We think it is important that our tone be welcoming and not demanding. We are likely to say any of the following: "Let's hear from everybody. A few of you have not yet spoken. Even though it is difficult to speak up, we hope you challenge yourself to do so." Members may choose to share relatively little about events outside of the group, yet they can still actively participate by keeping themselves open to being affected by others in the group, and they can share this.[6]

1. What would help you choose to speak about yourself if you were a member of a group?

_____

_____

_____

_____

[5] For a more detailed discussion of using dyads, see _Group Techniques_ (Chapter 4).

[6] For a more detailed discussion of guidelines and suggestions for orienting members to a group, see _Group Techniques_ (Chapter 3). See also the section on helping members get the most from a group experience, and the section on group norms at the initial stage, in _Groups: Process and Practice_ (Chapter 6).

2. At the initial session a group member says to you, "I really don't have anything to say now, and I don't want to be forced to participate." What would you say to this person?

_____

_____

_____

3. What would you say to a quiet member who tells you that in his or her culture it is considered impolite to speak up without being specifically asked to talk?

_____

_____

_____

Shared Responsibility

VIEW VIDEO SECTION 4: SHARED RESPONSIBILITY

As leaders, we do not want to be the only ones working, nor do we want members to rely on us to consistently bring them into the interactions. A few examples from the video illustrate how we build a norm of shared responsibility. Marianne invites Jackie to bring herself into the group process after Jackie says, "If I bring myself in when someone else is talking, my fear is that I would interrupt what's going on." The coleaders teach members how to best include themselves in what may be happening in the group at a given point. We tell members that they are not as likely to interfere with the group process if they share how they are affected at that moment by what is going on. Thus we encourage Jackie to take the risk of possibly interrupting an interaction rather than sitting in the group quietly while she waits for her turn to speak. We are trying to shape the norm for members to spontaneously enter into interactions when the current issue has meaning to them, rather than to rely on us to draw them in.

We teach members to take an active role in the process of monitoring what they are feeling, thinking, and doing. We do not want them to expect that we will know and point out when they are feeling scared, intimidated, or withdrawn. A few examples illustrate this point. James says he feels he has to prove himself. We want James to monitor specific times during the sessions when he becomes aware of striving to prove himself. We ask Jackie, who is aware of the authority figures (coleaders), to pay attention to the times when the presence of Marianne and Jerry might get in her way of doing work. Casey says she fears being vulnerable and that she rehearses endlessly before finally speaking, and we encourage her to speak up when she experiences feelings of vulnerability. Casey can accomplish this by simply announcing that she feels vulnerable and that she is rehearsing.

Casey is a good example of a member who is in the habit of censoring her expression of thoughts and feelings. She is afraid of being inappropriate or being judged if she voices what she is thinking. We hope she will learn that this group is a safe place to discover what would happen if she more frequently says out loud what she is thinking and feeling, which is one of her stated goals.

1. What would you most want to accomplish at the initial stage of a group?

_____

_____

_____

2. What member most stood out for you thus far, and why?

_____

_____

_____

3. How would you encourage members to assume shared responsibility for the direction of the group?

_____

_____

_____

Role Plays

VIEW VIDEO SECTION 5: ROLE PLAYS

We frequently use role plays to have members show us how they struggle with a particular relationship rather than report stories about problematic relationships. We ask members to identify specific individuals in the group who could represent significant others and who could be helpful to them in furthering their work. Routinely, we instruct them not to talk about an issue, but to make it present by speaking directly to another person during a symbolic role play. Darren identifies people who could assist him as he explores his feelings of "being a young kid." He selects Andrew and James to be his older brothers and Jerry to be his father. By bringing a conflict into the present, we get a much better understanding of how Darren struggles with feeling young. Role-playing techniques facilitate a deeper understanding and insight, a greater emotional connection, and tend to draw others into the work by tapping into their own emotions. Engaging in a role play and symbolically reliving some painful experiences tends to help members release pent-up emotions and can be a catalyst for the beginning of a healing process. Experiential methods, such as role playing, enable participants to attend to unfinished business from the past and to find a different ending to a painful event. Members often are able to make a new decision about a particular life situation. When a conflict situation is enacted, members also have opportunities to practice more productive ways of relating to others.[7]

Reflect on these questions from the vantage point of you being a group leader.

1. What purpose do you see in asking members to engage in role playing, even at the early sessions?

_____

_____

_____

2. How would you introduce a role play?

_____

_____

3. Assume you ask Darren to role-play and talk to his brother and he tells you, "I think role playing is silly. I'd rather just tell you about my brother and how we just don't get along." How would you deal with that?

_____

_____

_____

4. What would you say to a member who interrupts another member's role play by asking questions?

_____

_____

_____

---

[7] For an in-depth discussion of role-playing techniques, see *Theory and Practice of Group Counseling* (Chapter 8, Psychodrama).

Here and Now

We consistently ask members to pay attention to their present reactions to and perceptions about one another. For a group to achieve a genuine level of trust, it is essential that they express persistent reactions that pertain to what is going on in the context of the group. We underscore the importance of members saying what is on their mind, even though they fear that they may interrupt what is going on. When members keep their reservations to themselves, there is no way that we can deal with their concerns. When participants share certain reactions that could get in their way of participating fully in the group, we have a basis to do some productive work. For instance, Jackie lets us know that she will probably feel intimidated by us as authority figures because she never feels good enough. She also shares that she tends to be cautious as a way to avoid hurting anyone's feelings or creating a conflict. With this information now being public, she is in a good position to use reactions that will emerge for her as a reference point for some intensive work.

We are interested in both a here-and-now focus and a there-and-then focus. However, we find that members are usually not ready to take the risk of dealing with significant personal issues outside the group until they first deal with their reactions to one another in the room. When members bring up either a present or past problem situation from outside of the group, we explore how this might be played out in the context of the present group. For example, James says that he often feels that he has to prove himself at work. Both Jacqueline and Jackie inform us how much they are seeking approval. Andrew talks about feeling isolated. All these members are asked to take note when they experience these feelings or thoughts in the group.

We emphasize members' here-and-now reactions, but we also ask them to explore how their present reactions in the group may reflect how they feel away from the group. Jackie expresses her concern that she will not live up to our expectations, nor will she get our approval. Eventually, as the group becomes more established, we hope Jackie will also increase her awareness of how her struggles operate in her everyday life.

1. As a *member*, what difficulties might you experience if the leader emphasizes a here-and-now focus?

_____

_____

_____

2. As a *leader*, what might you say or do to promote a here-and-now focus in your groups?

_____

_____

_____

Making Contracts
VIEW VIDEO SECTION 6: MAKING CONTRACTS

As members state what they want to accomplish, we routinely ask them if they are willing to take the steps necessary to reach their goals. We also check to determine that the goals they are setting for themselves represent what they want, rather than goals they feel pressured to accept from someone else. Casey reports that she wants to rehearse and edit less, and express herself more often. She agrees to make a contract to more spontaneously express her inner thoughts. Marianne wonders if Casey's desire to challenge her own cultural injunctions is indeed her own agenda. She asks, "How come you want to change this?" Later in the group, Jerry suggests some work to Casey. When Casey hesitates, Marianne again asks Casey whether this is her agenda or Jerry's.[8]

---

[8] For a more detailed discussion of preparing contracts, see *Group Techniques* (Chapter 3).

1. How would you use contracts with a group you are leading? How would you help members design their contract?

_____

_____

_____

2. If you were a member of this group, how open would you be in agreeing to make a contract?

_____

_____

_____

Direct Talk

VIEW VIDEO SECTION 7: DIRECT TALK

Rather than have members talk *about* a concern they mention, we consistently ask them to select someone in the group to talk with directly. Members have a tendency to talk about an individual in the group. When this occurs we instruct them to look at and talk directly to that person. For example, Jyl reveals that she is feeling very exposed. When people feel exposed, they are usually aware of someone noticing them, and thus Marianne inquires, "Whom do you notice?" After Jyl indicates that James is the one she notices, she is asked to look at James, speak directly to him, and tell him what she is experiencing.

1. What does it say about members when they talk directly to another person as opposed to talking about that person?

_____

_____

_____

2. If you were a *leader* in this group, what cultural factors would you be sensitive to before asking members to speak directly to one another?

_____

_____

_____

Look and See

VIEW VIDEO SECTION 8: LOOK AND SEE

Throughout the duration of a group, we ask members to look at those with whom they are having reactions or making assumptions about. Jyl assumed that James was judging her; however, when she looked at him as she spoke to him, she began to see acceptance rather than judgment. Jyl would have missed that had she directed her eye contact away from James. With this Jyl becomes aware of her projections. Jacqueline indicates that she feels marginalized as an African American woman and sometimes feels different around Euro-Americans. If she agrees, we ask Jacqueline to look around the group and become aware of her reactions. We could have her address individuals by indicating some of the ways she feels different from them.

1. What therapeutic value do you see in asking a member to make eye contact with another person in the group as she or he is talking about a problem area?

_____

_____

_____

2. If a member said that he had a difficult time in selecting a person to talk to directly and to make eye contact with because in his culture doing this is considered rude, how would you respond?

Avoiding Quick Solutions

Rather than providing quick solutions, it is essential that members have an opportunity to express their feelings and thoughts. When a member raises self-doubts, fears, or struggles, we block other members from offering reassurance before this individual has had an opportunity to explore his or her concern. When Jyl is crying as she is talking to James, we do not facilitate members giving her reassurance or telling her that she has no reason to feel embarrassed. Instead, when Jyl says she feels exposed, our intervention leads her to say more about what it is like for her to feel exposed. Although quick reassuring feedback from members may make her feel good for a brief moment, it is doubtful that this feeling will be long-lasting. This is based on the assumption that Jyl's critic lies within her and not primarily with others.

1. Jyl cries and says she feels exposed. As a leader, how would you respond to her?

2. If you were leading this group, what are you likely to say to a member who asks Jyl many questions about why she feels embarrassed?

Dealing With Conflict

VIEW VIDEO SECTION 9: DEALING WITH CONFLICT

A group cannot achieve a genuine level of safety if conflict is brewing and is not addressed. Conflict may occur at any stage of a group. During the first session in this group, there was conflict between Jyl and James when she announced that she felt judged by him. Jyl's feelings were hurt when Jacqueline made the comment, "What I have to say is not very nice." Although Jyl did not let Jacqueline know how she was affected by her comment, it was crucial that the leader drew attention to Jacqueline's comment. Marianne, operating on her hunch that Jacqueline's comment did not register well with Jyl, asked Jyl what it was like to hear the remark. Jyl responded with, "Being me with you is not safe. I'm going to have to protect myself. The look on your face lets me know that I'm likely to be judged by you." Because both of them were willing to acknowledge the tension between them and continued talking, they were able to resolve the conflict, and they were able to again establish trust between them.

The same was true for Jyl and James. Another potential conflict situation was prevented when Jyl gave her reactions to both James and Jacqueline when they were talking about not being taken seriously because of their ethnicity. Jyl admits that she does not know what it's like to be an African American woman or an educated Chicano, yet she discloses how she struggles in a similar way when she says, "I know what it's like to be a white woman—an educated, white woman—who is sometimes treated like a piece of fluff." These examples show that conflict does not have to be divisive, if all who are involved express their reactions and continue the dialogue. It is crucial that the leaders are alert to subtle conflict that may be brewing and teach members how to deal with one another. Leaders should not collude with members to avoid conflict; instead, they need to model that it is safe to address an interpersonal conflict, and that the conflict can be productively resolved. During the early stages of a group, the members are keenly aware of ways that conflict is being dealt with by the leaders and between members. If conflict is not addressed adequately, it is likely to have a significant impact on the trust and cohesion of the group at a later phase of development.

Reflect on these questions from the vantage point of being a leader of this group.

1. How might the way you deal with conflict in your personal life help or hinder you as a leader in dealing with conflict in groups?

2. What would you do if you sense a conflict is emerging in the group, yet members deny that there is any tension?

3. How would you respond to Jacqueline when she makes the comment, "What I have to say would not be nice."

4. Would you be likely to draw attention to Jacqueline's remark? Why or why not?

What Will Get in Your Way in This Group?

VIEW VIDEO SECTION 10: WHAT WILL GET IN YOUR WAY IN THIS GROUP?

We teach members to speak up, even if they have not yet formulated exactly what they want to say. We often say, "It is easy to let an entire session go by without speaking up. The longer you wait to involve yourself, the more difficult it will become. Challenge yourself to say something at the beginning of each group, even if it's a brief statement of what it is like for you to come to group today." Members often discover if they force themselves to express even briefly something that is on their mind as they come to a session, this will make it easier to become more involved. It is especially useful for members to monitor their internal dialogue and any hesitations they may have about participation and vocalize this.

Early in the course of a group we typically ask participants to reflect on what they are likely to do that will interfere with what they want from the group experience. We say something like, "What will you do when you become anxious? How might you hold back? How could you sabotage yourself? What are you willing to do when you recognize that you are getting in your own way?" As coleaders, we don't assume responsibility to point out their avoidances. Instead, we encourage members to monitor what they are doing and call themselves on self-defeating behavior during the group.

When we asked members in the group to reflect on the questions listed in the previous paragraph, they readily identified some ways they could avoid speaking when they got scared. Below are some examples:

ANDREW: I'll edit myself by trivializing. I tell myself that what I have to say is not that important. I'll let others talk and convince myself that they have more significant issues.

CASEY: I rehearse. I'm afraid I can't articulate my thoughts well enough for you to understand me. I want to sound intelligent. Because I think I have to be perfect, I may not let you know what I'm thinking.

JACQUELINE: I'm afraid I won't say things well. I beat myself up after a group. I tell myself that I didn't say what I wanted clearly enough.

JACKIE: I try hard not to react. I realize when I'm hurt, but it is hard to say "ouch."

DARREN: I feel young and invisible. I don't know how to get in with you guys, so I'm likely to withdraw.

JAMES: You won't know when I feel outside the group because I won't tell you. I hold back.

JYL: When I get scared or feel like I'm being judged, I'll retreat.

SusANNE: I'm afraid my problem will be so big that I won't be able to handle it. My first instinct is to disappear.

During the initial phase of a group, members typically appear somewhat hesitant to get involved. For example, we don't view SusAnne's statement as mere avoidance. Her hesitation may be related to a lack of trust in the leaders or the members to be able to handle a problem that she brings forth. Members may be intimidated by the leaders or by certain other members, and they are sizing up one another. Some initial hesitation can be expected. How any early signs of resistance are dealt with by the leaders is important. Because we recognize that members are anxious, and that this anxiety can be used therapeutically, we begin by encouraging the members to share and explore their reactions.

As coleaders, what we are likely to say to these members collectively is something like the following: "When you become anxious in this group, you are likely to behave exactly as you just described. I hope you call yourself on your behavior when you notice that you are avoiding. I may or may not notice it, so I need your help. When you get scared and withdrawn, push yourself to announce your reactions. Doing so will allow us to work together and give you an opportunity to do something different. Note what might happen if you behave in new ways when you find yourself becoming anxious."

1. Imagine you are coleading this group. Pick one of the member's statements above and write your response to him or her.

_____

_____

_____

2. Assume you are a *member* of this group. In what ways might you sabotage yourself from getting what you want from the group? What would help you to challenge yourself?

_____

_____

_____

3. As a member, what would make you most anxious during an early session? How are you likely to deal with your anxiety?

_____

_____

_____

4. What other strategies can you think of to address a member's hesitation and/or avoidance?

_____

_____

_____

A Coleadership Style

By this time, you have noticed our style of interacting with each other, and with the members, as coleaders. We value coleading because it affords many opportunities for modeling the points we want to teach group members. The participants will learn more from how we behave in group sessions than by what we tell them. We suggest that you look for specific lessons that can be drawn from what you see of our co-facilitation style. As much as possible, we strive to be natural and spontaneous in our joint work. We do not decide beforehand who will say what or who will make what intervention. In fact, there are times when we may have different ideas about how to pursue work with an individual member or different perceptions about initiating work in the group as a whole. At these times we simply talk out loud about our perceptions. From our vantage point, it is essential that you have a basic respect for, and trust in, your coleader. You can have different styles of leadership, and these differences can even enhance your work together. It is important to make time to meet with your coleader and to talk about your leading together.[9]

1. What advantages do you see in working with a coleader?

2. What potential disadvantages might there be in working with a coleader?

3. What are some specific things you are noticing about the way the coleaders work together?

COREYS' COMMENTARY: THE INITIAL STAGE

The initial phase of the group is a time for members to get to know one another. It is difficult to build a climate of safety if members do not have a sense of one another. It is not our intention to have members immediately focus on exploring their deeper personal issues at the first meeting, but to heighten their awareness of the atmosphere in the room. This is a time for orientation, getting acquainted, learning how the group functions, developing the norms that will govern the group, exploring fears and expectations pertaining to the group, identifying personal goals, and determining if this group is a safe place. The manner in which the leader deals with the reactions of members determines the degree of trust that can be established in the group.

In these early sessions we are shaping specific group norms (working in the here and now, talking directly to one another, expressing persistent reactions, dealing with expectations and fears, establishing personal goals, and so on). Our main attention is on establishing a foundation of trust. We do this by getting members to talk about afterthoughts, by teaching them how to pay attention to what they are experiencing in the here and now, and by noticing their reactions to others in the group and getting members to verbalize these reactions. Notice that we do considerable teaching about how the participants can most productively involve themselves in the ongoing group process.

---

[9] For a more detailed discussion of the coleadership model, see *Groups: Process and Practice* (Chapter 2), with attention to the advantages and disadvantages of coleading. For ideas of possible lines group leaders can use at the various stages of a group, see *Student Manual for Theory and Practice of Group Counseling* (Chapters 4 and 5). Chapter 2 of the manual contains guidelines for meeting with your coleader. As a basis for discussion with your coleader, you might want to use the self-evaluation of group leader skills in Chapter 2 of the manual. In *Theory and Practice of Group Counseling* (Chapter 2) there is a section on coleading groups.

SUMMARY OF THE INITIAL STAGE

Basic Characteristics of the Initial Stage. The early phase of a group is a time for orientation and determining the structure of the group. Some of the distinguishing events of this stage are as follows:

- Participants test the atmosphere and get acquainted.
- Members learn the norms and what is expected, learn how the group functions, and learn how to participate in a group.
- Risk-taking is relatively low, and exploration is tentative.
- Group cohesion and trust are gradually established if members are willing to express what they are aware of in the here and now.
- Members are concerned with whether they are included or excluded, and they are beginning to define their place in the group.
- A central issue is safety and being assured of a supportive atmosphere.
- Members may look for direction and wonder what the group is about.
- Members are deciding who they can trust, how much they will disclose, how safe the group is, who they are drawn to and with whom they feel distant, and how much to get involved.
- Members are learning the basic attitudes of respect, empathy, acceptance, caring, and responding—all attitudes that facilitate trust building.

Member Functions. Early in the course of the group, these specific member roles and tasks are critical to shaping the group:

- Taking active steps to create a trusting climate
- Learning to express one's feelings and thoughts, especially as they pertain to here-and-now interactions in the room
- Being willing to express fears, hopes, concerns, reservations, and expectations concerning the group
- Being willing to make oneself known to others in the group
- Being involved in the creation of group norms
- Establishing individual goals that will govern group participation
- Learning how groups work and how to best participate in the process

Leader Functions. The major tasks of group leaders during the orientation and exploration phase of a group are as follows:

- Teaching participants the basics of group process
- Developing ground rules and setting norms
- Assisting members in expressing their fears and expectations and working toward the development of trust
- Modeling the facilitative dimensions of therapeutic behavior
- Being open with members and being psychologically present for them
- Showing members that they have a responsibility for the direction and outcome of the group
- Providing a degree of structuring that will neither increase member dependence nor promote excessive floundering
- Helping members establish concrete personal goals
- Dealing openly with members' concerns and questions
- Teaching members basic interpersonal skills such as active listening and responding
- Assessing the needs of the group and facilitating in such a way that these needs are met[10]

---

[10] For a discussion of group characteristics at the initial stage, group process concepts, and leader functions at the initial stage, see *Groups: Process and Practice* (Chapter 6). For a discussion of characteristics of the initial stage and techniques appropriate for the initial stage, see *Group Techniques* (Chapter 4). For a summary of issues pertaining to the early stages of a group's development, see *Theory and Practice of Group Counseling* (Chapter 4, text and student manual). For a discussion of applying different theoretical perspectives in working with themes emerging from the group, see *Theory and Practice of Group Counseling* (Chapter 17, text and student manual).

QUESTIONS FOR APPLYING THE SUMMARY LIST

Now that you have watched this segment of the group during its initial stages, apply the summary list from the previous page to the following questions concerning the group.

1. What theoretical orientations do you see in action in the early stage of this group?

_____

_____

_____

2. What are some specific group counseling techniques that you most noticed in the first sessions?

_____

_____

_____

3. If you were coleading, what would you most want to talk with your coleader about at this point in your group's development?

_____

_____

_____

IN-CLASS EXERCISE: QUESTIONS FOR SMALL GROUP DISCUSSION AND REFLECTING TEAMS

Form reflecting teams in small groups within your class. After viewing the initial stage of this group, share your observations and reactions. It is important for you to avoid judging, diagnosing, and interpreting. For instance, avoid labeling a member as being "emotionally restricted" or trying to figure out the dynamics between individuals. In your small group, focus on what you heard and saw, on the interactions that stood out for you, and the most salient moments during the initial stage of this group. The aim of the reflecting team is to share your thoughts, feelings, and reactions to what you are seeing unfold in the group and to reflect on your experience of observing the group in action. Pay particular attention to how you are personally affected by the members and the leaders and how that might influence the way you would lead this group.

1. During the early phase of a group, what kinds of norms would you be most interested in introducing to a group?
2. What would you want to teach members about how to get the most from one of your groups? How might you best teach members to make full use of the group experience?
3. What are your thoughts on how to encourage members to assume a share of the responsibility for the direction a group takes? How would you facilitate willingness on the part of participants to actively participate?
4. How ready are you to introduce role-playing activities in your groups?
5. How would you promote trust in your groups?
6. What kind of behaviors do you most want to model for the members of your groups?
7. What would you have learned about yourself had you been a member of a group such as this one? If you had been a leader?
8. What ethical issues can you identify concerning this segment of the group?
9. What qualities would you look for in your coleader?

Part III: The Transition Stage

SELF-INVENTORY

Directions: Complete this brief self-inventory before viewing the transition stage of the group. The purpose of the self-inventory is to help you identify and clarify your attitudes and beliefs about the variety of group process concepts, techniques, and issues in group leadership. The statements on the inventory are not simply right or wrong, true or false. The point is to get you in an active frame of mind as you watch and reflect on the video and as you complete the workbook activities. Your task is to decide the degree to which you agree or disagree with these statements. Then, after viewing this segment, look over your responses to see whether you want to modify them in any way.

Using the following code, write next to each statement the number of the response that most closely reflects your viewpoint:

5 = I strongly *agree* with this statement.
4 = I *agree*, in most respects, with this statement.
3 = I am *undecided* in my opinion about this statement.
2 = I *disagree*, in most respects, with this statement.
1 = I strongly *disagree* with this statement.

_____ 1. If a member displays reluctance to participate, or if there is a lack of participation in the group, this is a sure sign that the group leader is doing something wrong.

_____ 2. Conflict among members indicates that there is not an adequate degree of trust in the group.

_____ 3. If conflict were to arise, I would use techniques to shift the focus to something more constructive.

_____ 4. If a member were to say, "I feel that people will judge me," my intervention would be to ask members to give this person immediate positive feedback as a way to offer the member reassurance.

_____ 5. If members are hesitant and cautious, I think they need to be confronted immediately so this won't become a pattern.

_____ 6. I would confront members with care and respect, even if they say things to me that are difficult to hear.

_____ 7. I expect the groups I lead to be composed of members who may be hesitant and scared of interaction.

_____ 8. In leading a group, I think support needs to be balanced with challenge.

Building Safety

VIEW VIDEO SECTION 11: BUILDING SAFETY

Safety is a factor throughout the duration of a group. Establishing trust becomes even more important before a member is ready to engage in some deeper work. This group had established some degree of trust, yet all members were not at the same level. For example, SusAnne initiates some exploration of ways that she protects herself from being hurt with a wall. At some point during this discussion, Jerry asks her, "Do you think we will care about you enough to listen to you as you talk about your hurt?" SusAnne hesitates and then lets us know that she has doubts about our interest in her. Because of this, we do not facilitate the work SusAnne initiated, but our interventions are aimed at getting SusAnne to establish the level of safety in the room that will be necessary for her to pursue deeper self-exploration.

Another teaching point we want to make pertains to the metaphor of the *wall* that SusAnne mentions. We may return to her metaphor for further exploration at a later session. There are many useful interventions we could make, and which intervention we choose has a great deal to do with the clues we pick up from SusAnne. She gives us a sense of what direction she wants to move, and then we build upon that. Depending on what emerges into SusAnne's awareness, we might move in a number of different directions as we work with the metaphor of her wall. Some of these interventions are:

- "Describe this wall for us."

- "Let yourself become this wall, and talk to each of us individually about what it is like for you as the wall."

- "Talk to us about what this wall does for you in your life. How does it help you? What functions does it serve? How might your wall get in your way in life? How do you imagine life would be if you did not have this wall? Are you willing to take the wall down a bit in this group?"

We would not ask all of these questions, nor make all of these interventions. The above represents a sample of some of the ways we might assist SusAnne in exploring what her wall means to her and the potential price she is paying for keeping her wall. It is not up to anyone in the group to decide that she should tear down the wall, for that is her decision. Instead, we want to create a safe climate that will allow her to explore the meanings of her metaphor.

In our view, there is not one right way to intervene when members identify a problem area they want to explore. There are no perfect words, and there is no such thing as a perfect intervention. Depending on your style of group leadership, your theoretical orientation, and your perception of the context of what is going on in the group, you are likely to intervene in any number of ways. There are many fruitful ways to pursue therapeutic work that a client initiates. It is important to have an understanding of what you want to accomplish, and that this is in harmony with what your client wants to achieve. Although you won't know the outcome of a therapeutic experiment before it unfolds, you should have a rationale for your interventions.[11]

1. If SusAnne declared she wanted to take down her protective wall, what assumptions are you likely to make about what this means?

_____

_____

_____

2. What intervention might you make with SusAnne, and what would you most hope to accomplish with it?

_____

_____

_____

3. What theoretical orientation would you draw from in your work with SusAnne? Explain.

_____

_____

_____

Linking the Work of Members

VIEW VIDEO SECTION 12: LINKING THE WORK OF MEMBERS

One of the unique advantages of group counseling is that clients can learn from one another. Although some individual work in a group is useful, it is a better utilization of time and resources to involve several members. In this area the leaders help the group to identify common themes emerging within the group interactions. We want to create the norm that members can take the initiative to link themselves with others and not rely exclusively on the leaders to join them with others. One way for coleaders to link members is to pay attention to nonverbal reactions of members, as is seen in the program segment described below.

---

[11] For a detailed example and discussion of techniques used to explore a member's theme, "I don't feel safe in here," see *Group Techniques* (Chapter 5). An illustration of working with a member's theme, "I feel very burdened," is described in the same book (Chapter 6).

You will notice that Andrew has a dilemma of wanting to be safe versus reaching out to others. He wants to appear strong and is afraid that others will see him as being weak. During Andrew's work, Marianne notices that Jyl is tearing up. The coleaders involve Jyl by asking her to tell Andrew how he affects her. Both Andrew and Jyl can be engaged in a therapeutic dialogue. It is not necessary to drop Andrew in order to include Jyl. This is an example of enhancing one member's work by including others in the therapeutic exchange. The skill of linking is essential to maximize the therapeutic power inherent in a group.

Earlier Andrew mentioned that Jerry reminds him of his dad. Andrew now shares that he is feeling very self-conscious around Jerry because he does not want to appear weak. Marianne asks Andrew to express his feelings directly to Jerry, which he does. Jerry discloses to Andrew that he was tearing up and says, "What a shame that you have to surround yourself with a huge wall." Jerry's response was nothing close to what Andrew feared he might be thinking about him.

The reactions Jyl and Jerry shared toward Andrew did not confirm his feared hypothesis that people would not respect him if he let his guard down. Instead, he felt acknowledged and supported, which provided him with reinforcement to reveal more of the side of himself that he has locked up inside.

Andrew's dilemma of staying locked up versus needing others is a catalyst for others. James is drawn into Andrew's exchange with Jyl and with Jerry. James says, "I can identify with you. It takes a lot for me to feel I always have to be strong. I'd like to be able to tell my brother and father that it is OK to be weak." With this connection, we could invite James to talk more to Andrew, telling him what it is like to have to be strong all the time. By working together, both Andrew and James can make a decision about wanting to continue to live their lives as they have, or if they want to modify some aspect. Another way we could facilitate interaction would be to have James talk to Andrew as his brother, telling him ways he would like their relationship to be different. The symbolic role play that James would do with his brother could also be enlightening to Andrew.

From these examples, you can see how it is possible to bring several members into a piece of therapeutic work by linking their common struggles. Even though their stories may be different, they can be linked with the common pain they experience. Jyl, who was emotionally moved by Andrew's work and felt connected to him, later did an extensive piece of work with her own father. Even though we shift our attention from member to member, we avoid doing so at any member's expense. For instance, we notice Jyl crying and we ask her to tell Andrew, who was the focus of our attention, what she is experiencing. Linking her to Andrew makes it possible for us to attend to both individuals. If members are having emotional reactions to Andrew, more often than not, his struggle has some personal meaning to them. Neither Jyl nor James, in the process of telling Andrew how he affects them, are distracting from his exploration.

1. If Andrew declared he was tired of feeling locked up and wanted to be different, how would you pursue work with him?

_____

_____

_____

2. What outcome would you want to see in a role-playing situation involving Andrew and his symbolic father?

_____

_____

_____

3. What advantages do you see in linking members' agendas as you pursue work in a group, rather than focusing on one member at a time?

_____

_____

_____

"How Was the Day?"

VIEW VIDEO SECTION 13: "HOW WAS THE DAY?"

With any type of group we are leading, we set aside some time to ask members how the session was for them. Specifically, here are some areas we cover with this group: "How was the day for you? In what ways do you feel any different now than you did at the beginning of the day? Do you have any regrets about anything you did or said? How safe does the room feel to you now? What specifically do you want to bring up tomorrow?" At this juncture, we are interested in bringing closure to this session and getting members focused on how they can involve themselves in the upcoming session. Here are a few of the members' comments as well as our thoughts:

JAMES: "I was moved and I didn't expect that. I feel a little naked."

(What does he mean by feeling naked? Does he have regrets? We would encourage him to bring this up either now or at the beginning of the next session.)

SUSANNE: "I'd like to work on issues."

(This is a global statement that doesn't tell us much. We ask her to specify the issues and she responds with "trust issues." This is still vague, so we ask again and finally she identifies intimate relationships with males.)

JACKIE: "I feel a lot safer now. Tomorrow, I would like to work on my feeling inadequate."

(We ask her to reiterate what she did to bring about this increased safety. And we ask her to briefly identify if there was a time today when she felt inadequate and, if so, at what point.)

JACQUELINE: "I was surprised at the work I did today."

(In one sentence, we ask her to identify what was most surprising to her.)

Let us stress that this is not the time to get into an extensive discussion, but a time for wrapping up a few significant events. Here we are attempting to get members to be more specific and to give one-sentence replies. We can also get a commitment from members at this time if they are willing to bring up a certain issue in the following session. In general, the members perceived the room as a safer place and gave indications of being willing to talk out loud about what they are thinking and feeling. With this willingness to make themselves known, we feel hopeful about the progress of the group.

1. What would you want to focus on during the end of a group session?

_____

_____

2. Of the comments by SusAnne, Jackie, Jacqueline, and James, which one of them most catches your interest and why? What would you say to this person?

_____

_____

3. In the closing minutes of a group, assume that a member says she feels cut off by you. What would you say or do?

_____

_____

4. Assume a member says, "I didn't feel that we accomplished anything today. I was bored but didn't say anything for fear of offending anyone." How would you respond?

_____

_____

_____

OPENING AND CLOSING A GROUP SESSION

Checking-In Process. As you can see from the video, we make interventions to help members focus on how they can best involve themselves in each group session. We don't simply zero in on the first member who speaks, without first giving everyone a chance to participate in a check-in process. Typically, we expect all members to participate in a brief go-around so that we are able to create a tentative agenda based on the common concerns of members. Sometimes we structure the check-in by asking members to each address a specific question. Here are a few examples of ways to start a group session:

- What do you want for yourself from this particular session?
- Do any of you have thoughts or unfinished business from last week's session that you want to bring up now?
- What were you aware of as you were getting ready to come to group?
- Have you thought about anything that you explored at the last session?
- Would each of you be willing to complete the following sentence, "Right now I am aware of . . ."

1. What specific leadership skills are essential in the opening of a group session?

_____

_____

_____

2. What is the most important thing you hope to accomplish with the checking-in process?

_____

_____

_____

Checking-Out Process. You'll notice in the video that at the end of a day (a series of sessions for this particular group) we asked members to participate in a check-out process by saying how the day was for each of them. We ask them to identify some of the highlights of the sessions, and verbalize any topics they want to put on their agenda for the next session. We do not simply engage in intense work right up until the end of the session. Instead, we intervene in ways to assist members to bring closure on what they experienced. A few examples of questions we often use as catalysts for assisting members to say a few words about what has been most meaningful to them in a session follow:

- Are there any ways in which you'd like to be different in the next session than you were in this one?
- Even though we have been together for only a short time, what are you learning about yourself?
- Are you seeing any of your concerns reflected by others as they are talking?

We expect members to reflect on what is occurring within the group. We do not want to end abruptly, with little or no closure. Hearing even a few brief comments from every person provides the pulling together that is necessary as the group evolves.[12]

1. As a group leader, to what extent would you want to involve yourself in the check-out time during the closing of a session?

_____

_____

_____

---

[12] For a more detailed discussion of opening and closing group sessions, see *Groups: Process and Practice* (Chapter 6) and *Group Techniques* (Chapter 4). For ideas of possible lines group leaders can use at the initial stage, see *Student Manual for Theory and Practice of Group Counseling* (Chapter 4).

2. What strategies might you use to keep members' comments brief and to the point?

_____

_____

_____

COREYS' COMMENTARY: THE TRANSITION STAGE

Before groups progress to a working stage, they typically go through what we refer to as a transitional phase, which is characterized by anxiety, defensiveness, reluctance, the struggle for control, and intermember conflicts. During the transitional phase, it is the members' task to monitor their thoughts, feelings, and actions and to learn to express them verbally. In a respectful manner, leaders can help members come to recognize and accept their hesitations and reluctance yet, at the same time, push themselves to challenge their tendencies toward avoidance. For members to progress to a deeper level of exploration, it is necessary that they talk about any anxiety and reluctance they may be experiencing. Members make decisions regarding taking risks about bringing out into the open some ways they may be holding back, either out of what they might think of themselves or what others could think of them if they were to reveal themselves more. Some fears of members during an early stage and a transition stage, which are related to defensiveness, include the fear of rejection, losing control, being inappropriate, being involved in a conflict, or looking foolish. It is important that group leaders understand there is a purpose for any defense. Above all, member reluctance needs to be respected, understood, and explored.

Leaders should not attack reluctant members, but it is a mistake to bypass or ignore defensive behaviors. Some groups remain stuck at a transitional phase because members' nonproductive behaviors are unnoticed, ignored, or inadequately dealt with by the group leader. Teaching members how to challenge themselves is a basic task at this time, yet it is also essential that members learn how to respectfully confront others in a caring and constructive fashion. We teach members the importance of talking more about themselves and how they are affected by the behaviors of a member they are confronting, rather than telling a member how he or she is or judging that person. We hope we model how to remain open and nondefensive in receiving feedback from others. If conflicts arise, it is essential that members recognize these conflicts and develop the skills to resolve them. Again, what leaders model about addressing conflict in a respectful manner is every bit as important as what they tell members about conflict resolution. If conflict is not addressed, it becomes a hidden agenda, which blocks open group interaction. How group leaders intervene is crucial to the further building of trust.

During the initial stage, members generally address their fears or reservations about participating in the group. However, during the transition phase, there is a more extensive and specific discussion of how these fears are manifested within the group. Doing this enables members to feel the support and safety that is required for the intense work they are getting ready to do.

Checking In With Members

VIEW VIDEO SECTION 14: CHECKING IN WITH MEMBERS

We often open a new session, especially during the early phase of a group, with a brief dyad. This serves as a focusing exercise by assisting members to gain clarity on what they want from a particular session. We ask members to be responsible for what they want to bring up for exploration, rather than relying on us to determine their agenda. We also invite them to mention any unfinished business from the previous session. After participants have had a chance to talk in pairs for a few minutes, we reconvene as a group and each member declares a specific problem area he or she is ready to examine. We also typically add, "Is there anything in your awareness that keeps you from being present in this group at this moment?" We raise this question because sometimes members are distracted by something that has happened between sessions. Unless they take the opportunity to mention what is on their mind, full participation will likely be hindered.

During the check-in time, our aim is to hear what each person most wants to say briefly. We may stay with a member a bit longer to assist him or her in clarifying a goal or to solicit more information.

At times members become quite emotional as they describe a concern they want to address. In this case, we are apt to say, "Even as you describe your concern, it brings up a lot of feelings. I hope that after the check-in with everybody you will claim time to take care of yourself. Is it OK with you if we continue with our go-around right now?" We generally do not stay with any one member before we have completed the check-in process because we want all the members to have a chance to express what they are bringing to this session. Our aim is to identify common themes emerging within the group and to link the work of several members.

Here are some comments made by members in the video during the check-in time:

- Jyl mentions her tendency to isolate at times and adds that she would be disappointed if she did not do some work with her father.
- James says that he feels more present and closer to the group.
- Jackie declares that she would like to focus on her feelings of not being good enough.
- SusAnne again brings up her concerns pertaining to trust toward the group.
- Darren is feeling some energy with his dad. (Darren selects Jerry as a symbolic dad to work with later on.)
- Casey is afraid that people will judge her.
- Andrew states that he wants to explore his feelings of betrayal, his feelings of not being good enough, and how he keeps people out of his life. (Andrew picks Jyl as the person who could be helpful for him because both of them have issues with their fathers.)

During the check-in, Andrew mentions that he and Jyl have been talking between sessions. This kind of subgrouping between members does not have to be problematic as long as they are willing to bring into the group the essence of what transpired in their discussions. However, subgrouping is divisive when members discuss perceptions and reactions to others, yet fail to bring this to the entire group.

1. You are facilitating a check-in at the beginning of a meeting. Darren mentions that he wants to explore his relationship with his father, and he begins to cry. How would you handle this?

2. At the check-in Jyl says, "Last week I left feeling very disappointed. Even though I stated I wanted to talk about my father, we never got around to it. I felt cheated." What would be your response?

3. How would you handle the situation if you discovered that several members meet regularly between sessions?

Furthering of Trust Building

VIEW VIDEO SECTION 15: FURTHERING OF TRUST BUILDING

After each of the members has checked in, what we find interesting is the lack of trust that SusAnne feels in the group, especially since she has mentioned this before. Because this is a present, here-and-now reaction pertaining to the group, we encourage SusAnne to give expression to her level of trust in us. She informs us that she trusts us somewhat, but does not feel close. We ask her to address each of us individually and say something about the degree to which she trusts each person. Because SusAnne states that people might not be interested in her, we suggest that she address each group member by completing this statement: "You wouldn't be interested in me because . . . " She picked two people whom she felt she could trust, yet did not feel close to. Again, SusAnne was asked to talk to each of them individually and indicate how her feelings toward them might get in the way of her doing work. By acknowledging her doubts and fears, and by discussing them with individuals in the group, she was able to establish the trust necessary for her to get involved in some significant and intensive work later in the group.

Notice that we did not ignore SusAnne's reservations, nor did we encourage group members to offer reassurance to her that they were trustworthy. The core of the struggle lies within SusAnne, and she needs to decide if she is willing to take the risk of trusting the members. By making this decision out loud, she includes the people in the group with whom she has doubts. This process allows SusAnne to come to a greater realization of the projections she places on others. Eventually individuals can reply to SusAnne by letting her know whether her assumptions are indeed a reality from their vantage point. For instance, assume SusAnne says, "Marianne, you wouldn't be interested in me because you are too busy with everyone else." I might respond with, "Yes, I am busy, yet I am not too busy to be interested in you."

Creating Safety

VIEW VIDEO SECTION 16: CREATING SAFETY

As Casey begins to talk, she is looking down at the ground. She mentions that she worries about being judged by a couple of people. After asking her to select those people, she names SusAnne and Jacqueline. We direct Casey to talk out loud about the ways in which she fears these individuals might judge her. As she looks at both SusAnne and Jacqueline, Casey says aloud all the things she imagines they might be thinking about her. As leaders, we have a hunch that Casey is getting ready to make some deeper personal disclosures. Therefore, Casey first needs to deal with making the room safe, especially with these two people. As we did with SusAnne, we do not bypass nor ignore her reservations, rather we see this as a key focus of her work at this time. Again, we deal with Casey's fears and projections, rather than allowing members to reassure her that she has nothing to fear from them. This demonstrates how we work with members (SusAnne and Casey) to get them ready to do more intensive work at a later session.

Assume you are leading this group, which is in the transition stage, and SusAnne says, "I have a hard time trusting people in this group. I am afraid that people will judge me."

1. How would you respond to SusAnne's assumption that you would not be interested in her?

_____

_____

_____

2. How would you deal with members who felt rejected or offended by SusAnne's comment that she has a difficult time trusting people in the group?

_____

_____

_____

3. What intervention would you make if several other members joined in with SusAnne and stated that they too had difficulty trusting this group?

_____

_____

_____

COREYS' COMMENTARY: MORE ON THE TRANSITION STAGE

During the initial stage of a group, the feelings of safety and trust tend to be somewhat generalized. However, during the transition phase, members have had opportunities to observe others, form assumptions about with whom they have reservations, and have developed more intense projections toward others in the room. The anxiety is higher because members are beginning to take more risks by letting themselves be known on a deeper level. For example, it was essential that both SusAnne and Casey addressed here-and-now feelings to do the very intense therapeutic work that follows in later sessions. What took place in this session was a process of checking-in, making the room safe, talking about hesitations, and being more specific about what each member's agenda would be. This process of identifying and exploring what could hold members back is essential for a group to evolve into a deeper phase of interpersonal work. If there is a hidden agenda, such as unresolved conflicts, then members are not likely to engage in significant risk-taking.

No arbitrary dividing lines exist between the stages of a group. In actual practice these stages merge with each other. This is especially true of the movement from the transition stage to the working stage. The line between expressing anxieties and ways of avoiding, which is so characteristic of the transition stage, and of working through difficulties to move the group into a more advanced stage of development is not clearly marked. If a group does move into the working stage, it can be expected that earlier themes of trust, conflict, and reluctance to participate will surface from time to time. As a group takes on new challenges, deeper levels of trust have to be achieved. Also, considerable conflicts may be settled at the initial stage, yet new conflicts may emerge as the group evolves into the transition and working stages.

Even if a group reaches a working stage, all members may not be able to function at the same level of intensity. Some members may be on the periphery, others may still be cautious, and others may be less willing to take risks. Indeed, there are individual differences among members at all of the stages of a group. As you will see, some members may be very willing to engage in intensive emotional exploration, which can have the effect of drawing some of the more hesitant members into active participation.

SUMMARY OF THE TRANSITION STAGE

Basic Characteristics of the Transition Stage. The transitional phase of a group's development is marked by feelings of anxiety and defensiveness in the form of various problematic behaviors. At this time members:

- Wonder about others' acceptance or rejection of them
- Test the leader and other members to determine how safe the environment is
- Struggle with whether to remain on the periphery or to risk getting involved
- Experience some struggle for control and power and some conflict with other members or the leader
- Learn how to work through conflict and confrontation
- Feel reluctant to get fully involved in working on their personal concerns because they are not sure others in the group will care about them
- Observe the leaders to determine if they are trustworthy
- Learn how to express themselves so that others will listen to them

Member Functions. A central role of members at this time is to recognize and deal with the many forms of problematic behaviors. Tasks include:

- Recognizing and expressing the range of feelings
- Respecting one's own hesitations and ambivalences, but challenging oneself
- Taking increased responsibility for what they are doing in the group
- Learning how to confront others in a constructive manner
- Recognizing unresolved feelings from the past as they are being acted out in relation to the group leader or other members

- Being willing to face and deal with reactions toward what is occurring in the here-and-now group

- Being willing to work through conflicts rather than avoiding them

Leader Functions. Perhaps the central challenge that leaders face during the transition phase is the need to intervene in the group in a sensitive manner and at the appropriate time. The basic task is to provide both the encouragement and the challenge necessary for the members to face and resolve the conflicts that exist within the group and their own defenses against anxiety.

Some of the major tasks leaders need to perform during the transition phase include the following:

- Teaching group members the importance of recognizing and expressing their anxieties

- Helping participants recognize the ways in which they react defensively and creating a climate in which they can deal with their defenses openly

- Teaching members the value of recognizing and dealing openly with conflicts that occur in the group

- Providing a model for the members by dealing directly and honestly with any challenges to you as a person or as a professional

- Encouraging members to express reactions that pertain to here-and-now happenings in the sessions[13]

QUESTIONS FOR APPLYING THE SUMMARY LIST

Now that you have watched this segment of the group during its transitional stage, apply the above summary list to the following questions concerning the group.

1. As you observe the members at this stage of the group, what stands out most for you?

_____

_____

_____

2. What are you learning about how groups either function or malfunction at this point?

_____

_____

_____

3. What are the *main challenges* you expect to face at this stage in your group's development?

_____

_____

_____

IN-CLASS EXERCISE: QUESTIONS FOR SMALL GROUP DISCUSSION AND REFLECTING TEAMS

Form reflecting teams in small groups within your class. After viewing the transition stage of this group, share your observations and reactions. In your small group, focus on what you heard and saw, on the interactions that stood out for you, and the most salient moments during the transition

---

[13] For a discussion of the characteristics of a group at the transition stage, difficult group members, interventions for dealing with reluctance, and member and leader functions at the transition stage, see *Groups: Process and Practice* (Chapter 7). For a discussion of techniques for dealing with difficult members, dealing with conflict, exploring fears and reluctance, and working with challenges to leaders, see *Group Techniques* (Chapter 5). For a summary of issues pertaining to the transition stage of a group's development, see *Theory and Practice of Group Counseling* (Chapter 4, text and student manual). For a discussion of applying different theoretical perspectives in working with themes emerging from the group, see *Theory and Practice of Group Counseling* (Chapter 17, text and student manual).

stage of this group. The aim of the reflecting team is to share your thoughts, feelings, and reactions to what you are seeing unfold in the group and to reflect on your experience of observing the group in action. Pay particular attention to how you are personally affected by the members and the leaders and how that might influence the way you would lead this group. We suggest that you use your written responses to the Questions for Applying the Summary List as guidelines for your discussion in your reflecting team.

1. During the transition stage, members often express that they are holding back from expressing themselves. What ideas do you have that could lead to more open expression? How might members challenge themselves to say more of what they are thinking and feeling?

2. How ready are you to deal effectively with conflicts in a group situation?

3. What would you have learned about yourself had you been a member of a group such as this one? If you had been a leader?

4. What ethical issues do you need to be cognizant of concerning this segment of the group?

Part IV: The Working Stage

Directions: Complete this brief self-inventory before viewing the working stage of the group. The purpose of the self-inventory is to help you identify and clarify your attitudes and beliefs about the variety of group process concepts, techniques, and issues in group leadership. The statements on the inventory are not simply right or wrong, true or false. Decide the degree to which you agree or disagree with these statements. Then, after viewing this segment, look over your responses to see whether you want to modify them in any way. This self-inventory will help you express your views and will prepare you to think about the ideas you'll encounter in this section.

Using the following code, write next to each statement the number of the response that most closely reflects your viewpoint:

5 = I *strongly agree* with this statement.
4 = I *agree*, in most respects, with this statement.
3 = I am *undecided* in my opinion about this statement.
2 = I *disagree*, in most respects, with this statement.
1 = I *strongly disagree* with this statement.

_____ 1. A sign of a working stage involves the free interchange of the members without prodding from the leader.

_____ 2. If my group does not reach the working stage, I'll feel like I've failed the members and myself.

_____ 3. I associate the working stage with a great deal of emotional expression and catharsis.

_____ 4. I think there is a fine line between the transition and the working stage.

_____ 5. It is best if one member at a time works with the leader, rather than complicate things by having several members working simultaneously.

_____ 6. One of the more powerful ways to engage members in significant work is to ask them to role-play (or enact) a struggle in the group situation.

_____ 7. During the working stage, I would be the most active and directive as a leader.

_____ 8. The aim of the working stage should be to teach members problem-solving strategies.

Who Wants to Work?

VIEW VIDEO SECTION 17: WHO WANTS TO WORK?

When Jerry asks who wants to make use of the group time, James jumps in immediately. Although he says he wants time, he is ambivalent and attempts to shift the focus onto SusAnne, asking her to work in the hope that she will trigger his work. We intervene with this attempt. If James wants to work, he should not put another member on the spot. He then asks SusAnne if she is willing to role-play a former girlfriend, and she agrees. Even though James gets a green light from SusAnne and us, he hesitates, indicating that he jumped in too soon and that we should go to someone else. At this juncture, we are not invested in keeping the spotlight on James, who lets us know that he does not feel ready to proceed.

1. You are leading a group and ask, "Who wants to work?" There is a long silence and nobody gives any indication of wanting to work. What assumptions might you draw from this situation? What might you say?

_____

_____

_____

2. If none of the members bring up a concern they wish to explore, would you be inclined to call upon people? Why or why not?

_____

_____

_____

COMMENTARY ON CASEY'S WORK

VIEW VIDEO SECTION 18: COMMENTARY ON CASEY'S WORK

At this point, Casey indicates her eagerness to continue what she began in an earlier session, and we shift our focus to her. Casey is most aware of SusAnne and what she might think of her as she gets ready to make a significant disclosure. Casey acknowledges her projections about being judged negatively by SusAnne. Then Casey proceeds to tell SusAnne that she is gay.

Again, we can see how essential it is that Casey establishes a firm basis of trust in the room. She is taking a tremendous risk in disclosing that she is gay. At this point, she does not know how the people in the group will react to her, especially SusAnne and Jacqueline, whom she singled out earlier. Even though we may not say much to Casey as she is sharing, she needs to feel our presence and support. Later in her work, she acknowledged that she was aware of Marianne's presence, and that she felt supported. Although Casey feared judgments from the group members, she finds people to be very caring and accepting. We direct her to look around the room to ensure that this support registers with her, and we challenge her to remember what she sees in members' faces. Later on, should Casey slip into judging herself, we hope she can call to mind the supportive feedback she received from everyone.

Symbolic Exploration Through Role Playing

VIEW VIDEO SECTION 19: SYMBOLIC EXPLORATION THROUGH ROLE PLAYING

Casey's work takes a different turn when she expresses her sadness about having to keep her being gay a secret from her mother. Casey proceeds, yet is obviously frightened. Jerry suggests a role play involving Casey picking a person in the group to be her symbolic mother. We observe considerable hesitation on Casey's part. Marianne doesn't want Casey to feel pressured to move ahead with the role play and asks, "Is this your agenda or Jerry's?" She lets it be known that she is scared, yet she wants to continue. Casey agrees with Marianne that it would be more meaningful to role-play with her mother in her native language (Vietnamese). We continue to find that when people role-play with significant others in their primary language, the outcome of the therapeutic engagement is often more productive. It is not necessary that those in the room understand the content of what is being conveyed. What is important is that this therapeutic dialogue has meaning to the client. Those who observe the work are typically affected emotionally even though they do not understand what is being said.

Casey, who picks Marianne as her symbolic mother, first reveals that she is gay. We follow Casey's lead and she eventually says, "I keep thinking what my mother would say back to me." Marianne asks Casey to reverse roles, "becoming her mother," and express what she imagines her mother would tell her about this disclosure. After this exchange, Casey makes a comment about what a "good mother" would say. Again, taking the cue from Casey, Marianne suggests that Casey become the "good mother" and tell Marianne (who assumes the role of Casey) what she knows that Casey needs to hear.

In reality, Casey may never tell her mother about her sexual orientation, nor would we as coleaders ever push her to do so. What she tells her mother, if anything, must be her choice. Certainly, we would not tell Casey to go away from the group and say everything she expressed symbolically in the therapeutic situation. Instead, if she opens a dialogue with her mother, she needs to decide what she most wants to say to her, and what the price might be if she does. Even if Casey does not actually approach her mother, her therapeutic enactment was both cathartic and healing. Ideally, Casey would like to have the "good mother" she deserves, yet at this time, she made a start by symbolically saying to herself what she would so much like to hear from her mother. Casey's mother may never be able to agree with Casey's decisions of how she wants to live her life, yet Casey can come to an affirmation of herself as a person. A very important outcome of Casey's work was the realization that her catastrophic expectations (negative judgments from the members) were not based in reality. Marianne plants a seed in Casey's mind that maybe her mother, like the group, may not be as condemning of her as she fears. The stakes for Casey are high, and what to say to her mother will present some difficulties for her. Another result of her work was her decision to be a bit more trusting with select people about who she is.

Although the video contains a relatively large segment of Casey's therapy, the actual session lasted more than an hour. As can be seen, Casey's emotional work proves to be a catalyst for most of the other members. We, as leaders, were also emotionally touched, and generally we do not hesitate to disclose this. Just because we become emotional does not imply that we lose our objectivity and our ability to facilitate the members' interactions.[14]

1. What reactions did you have as you observed Casey's work with her mother? What aspects of her work most affected you, and why? How might your reactions help or hinder you in working with her?

_____

_____

_____

2. Assume that after Casey disclosed that she was gay one of the members said, "Casey, I need to let you know that I have a hard time hearing this, because I'm not comfortable with homo-sexuality." How would you intervene?

_____

_____

_____

3. In a role play, Casey spoke to her symbolic mother in Vietnamese? As she did so, what did you observe?

_____

_____

_____

4. What would you say if several group members began pressuring Casey to talk to her mother in real life and let her know about her sexual orientation?

_____

_____

_____

5. Marianne was emotionally affected by Casey's work, and let her know this. What would you do or say if you became emotionally involved in a member's work?

_____

_____

_____

Involving Other Members in Intensive Work

In later sessions every member did some emotionally laden work and engaged in significant and insightful self-exploration. Much of that work was triggered by the earlier work of others. Only brief

---

[14] For a more detailed illustration of using a member's native language in a symbolic role play, see *Group Techniques* (Chapter 6).

segments of some of the members' work can be seen in the video. On the following pages we highlight ways that other members brought themselves into the session by addressing their struggles.[15]

Jyl's Loss of Her Father

VIEW VIDEO SECTION 20: JYL'S LOSS OF HER FATHER

Some of Jyl's unfinished business with her father pertains to the fact that when she was growing up he communicated to her that she could never become the great pianist that she thought she could become. Instead, he waited until the day before he died to tell her that she could have made it. This leads Jyl to explore the possibility that it is not too late for her to resume her career as a pianist. One of Jyl's issues is that she tends to withdraw in social interactions. She gets the insight that she could use playing the piano as a way to reach out and make contact with others. Jyl makes a contract to do this before the follow-up session for this group.

1. How would you decide what to focus on with Jyl? Would you focus on her sadness over losing her father? Her issues with men? Her disappointment in not having become a pianist? What would guide you in your decision?

2. How might you work with Jyl's tendency to withdraw in social situations?

Never Good Enough

VIEW VIDEO SECTION 21: NEVER GOOD ENOUGH

Jackie is very affected as she talks about working so hard on being perfect and pleasing everybody, never making anyone mad, and never feeling like she is enough. During a go-around she explores how hard she tries to be entertaining, witty, funny, pretty, and never boring. As a result of her exploration in group, she realizes that she has always felt responsible for her mother's leaving, even at the age of 7. Although Jackie realizes on a cognitive level that she wasn't responsible for her mother leaving, on an emotional level she is still not convinced. Jackie's insights into her dynamics can help her to more readily recognize those instances when she exhausts herself by attempting to be everything to everybody.

1. Jackie talks about trying to please others and to be perfect. To what degree can you identify with her issue? How might this help or hinder you in facilitating her work?

2. Given that Jackie has insight into her behavior, would you be inclined to suggest homework to her, and if so, what would this be?

---

[15] For a description of working with several members who experience intense emotions in group sessions, see *Group Techniques* (Chapter 6).

Wanting Approval

VIEW VIDEO SECTION 22: WANTING APPROVAL

Jacqueline initially brought up her need for universal approval. In this session, she gets in touch with her pain over trying to connect with her mother, and getting her mother's approval. She role-plays with Marianne as her symbolic mother, which leads to insight regarding how she often expects people around her to approve of her in the way her mother never did.[16]

1. Jacqueline talks about striving to get her mother's approval. What strategies would you use to facilitate her work?

---

2. Discuss what you consider to be the pros and cons of the leader being utilized by group members in role plays.

Linking Members by Role Playing

During the group, but not shown in the video, James and Jackie engage in a very long role play in which Jackie symbolically talks to James as her son and James talks to Jackie as his mother. Both are helped by this role play. James has an opportunity to express some words he rarely says to his mother. Eventually, he contracts to spend some time with his mother and to tell her how much he appreciates her and cares for her. Jackie receives the longed-for recognition and appreciation that she so much desires from her son. She provides feedback to James, hoping that he will indeed talk to his mother, and lets James know how good it felt to hear his words. This interchange between Jackie and James illustrates how transference in groups, if tapped, can be productive in helping members explore places they are stuck in significant relationships. We pay close attention to transference and look for ways to link members who can be therapeutically useful to each other. Those symbolic enactments in the group frequently lead to a new direction in their interpersonal relationships outside of the group.

Working With Metaphors

VIEW VIDEO SECTION 23: WORKING WITH METAPHORS

We also pay close attention to words, phrases, and metaphors that members use to describe themselves. Darren is affected by the symbolic enactments with parental figures. He already has some insight into the parallels between his relationship with his parents and how he often feels with people in this group. He feels that his mother has a hard time in seeing him as an adult, and likewise, he sees himself in the group as a kid who tries to fit in. Darren says, "I wish I had more of a relationship with my parents. It gets in my way with people in this group. It feels like a 'hole in my soul.'" After he continues talking for a while, Marianne draws his attention to what appeared to be a significant phrase. Marianne says, "You said an important word. I experience it as a 'hole in my soul.' Do you want to look at a few people and repeat that sentence?"

Darren looks at different members and says, "It feels like a hole in my soul. I blame myself for it, like there is something wrong with me." As can be seen in the video, Darren gets intensely emotional as he taps into some painful childhood memories. He is crying and looking down at the floor. Marianne suggests that he pick a person who would be helpful for him to make contact with as he

---

[16] For a discussion of utilizing techniques in dealing with the theme, "I so much want your approval," see *Group Techniques* (Chapter 6).

continues talking. He picks Jyl and begins talking to her as Jyl, and then shifts and addresses her as his mother. Darren talks to Jyl, "I wish you could have been there for me." Marianne says, "Keep looking at her, even though it is hard."

Darren continues, "I had to do everything by myself. I was scared and lonely. I wanted to tell someone how I felt. I feel so alone with my feelings. And I still feel that way a lot. I don't know how to show my feelings." Marianne interjects, "You are showing a lot of feelings now." Darren looks at her and says, "Yes." He continues, "It was hard growing up that way." Marianne's comment is aimed at reinforcing Darren's expression of deep feelings because Darren just said that he is unable to do so. We often note and give members feedback when they are demonstrating a behavior that they claim they cannot do.

Typically, we ask members to look at and talk to a particular person in the group, whether or not that individual reminds them of a significant other. We want members to be aware of the supportive presence that is often in the room. This supportive connection generally enables them to take the risks involved in going to scary places, as was the case with Darren.

Jerry made an intervention as Darren was speaking, "How old do you feel now?" Darren picked about 7 years old. Jerry asks Darren to continue talking, but as the 7-year-old child. This gives us important information about Darren's experiences as a child and possible decisions he made at that time that are now interfering with his adult life. He is currently operating on old decisions, some of which are no longer functional. As a child he felt lonely, and now in this group he doubts that he fits in. This causes him to be hesitant with people in this group as well as in his outside life. Consequently, what he tells himself keeps him lonely. Because of this exploration, Darren becomes keenly aware that he expects people to treat him the way his family responded to him. With the awareness of how he sets up a self-fulfilling prophecy, he can begin to act differently. Instead of shying away from people, he can approach people with the attitude that he has something to offer them and that they might be interested in him.

As you notice in the video, Darren, as well as others, are encouraged to continue talking even though they are crying. It is therapeutic for members to put words to their emotions. There is a great deal of wisdom and truth expressed during moments such as these. We carefully listen to what Darren is saying while he is emotional in order to be able to reflect back and to remind him, at a later point, what he has said. We don't give him words or tell him what to feel. Instead, we pick up sentences and phrases that Darren has said and have him repeat those during a role-play situation, such as the phrase "hole in my soul." Darren reported that his father wasn't there for him. During a role play with his symbolic father, we might tell him to let his father know what it felt like to not have his father there.

Darren expresses a good deal of hurt toward his parents. At some point he suddenly interrupts himself, turns to Marianne and says, "My mom and dad did the best they could with what they had, but it still hurt growing up." We want to be respectful of Darren's needs to protect his parents at that moment. Furthermore, we are likely to discourage group members from talking him out of being understanding of his parents. Darren can be hurt, angry, understanding, and eventually, forgiving. It is important that he gives sufficient expression to his whole range of feelings. These symbolic role plays with parents go beyond blaming one's past for current problems. We see it as being therapeutically valuable to give expression to painful feelings associated with past and present events. Participants typically report a sense of release and healing after expressing bottled-up emotions. The emotional release, coupled with the insight that frequently follows, enables members to make new and more functional decisions about how they want to live.

After members experience a cathartic breakthrough, it is not uncommon for them to report their awareness of feeling exposed, embarrassed, naked, and vulnerable. At times like this, members sometimes discount the actual work they did and the courage they displayed. What is crucial at these times is to avoid giving quick reassurance, or attempting to talk members out of their feelings. For instance, Jerry asks Darren, "How was it for you to do this work?" Darren lets us know, "It was really hard. I feel that I showed my worst. I feel that I was weak." Now Jerry urges Darren to look at members in the room and to verbalize his concerns, especially what he fears that people might be thinking about him. Looking at people in the room, rather than turning away in embarrassment, enables Darren to note the understanding and compassion that others are feeling toward him. If he gets stuck with his embarrassment, he is likely to discount his insights and begin to criticize himself for "breaking down" in front of others. When Darren is being self-critical, Jerry asks him to reflect on what he thought about others who showed their emotions. Jerry slowly facilitates Darren toward giving himself the kind of understanding and nonjudgmental acceptance that he is willing to give to others.[17]

1. How were you affected as you observed Darren's work? How might that influence the way you work with him?

_____

_____

_____

2. How would you work with Darren's metaphor of feeling "It's like a hole in my soul"?

_____

_____

_____

3. Assume that after Darren's work he announces, "I'm feeling vulnerable and embarrassed. I can't believe that I lost control like that." How would you deal with this statement?

_____

_____

_____

Working With Relationships

VIEW VIDEO SECTION 24: WORKING WITH RELATIONSHIPS

Earlier SusAnne spent a considerable amount of time establishing trust with members. She was able to go beyond her reluctance, which was expressed by her lack of clarity and focus. Because she took care of these foundational concerns, she is now able to initiate and negotiate a role play with James as her former boyfriend. SusAnne declares that she keeps a lot of words and feelings inside, which causes her a great deal of physical stress. She agrees that it would be helpful to hear herself say out loud some of the things that she often pounds her head with silently. SusAnne not only verbalizes her pain in this role play with James as her boyfriend, but also is asked to symbolically hand over elements of her pain to him. She very deliberately hands over to him hurt, lies, shame, and guilt. Notice that after SusAnne has given away feelings she's held in, she declares that she feels much lighter, especially in her shoulders.

At this point it is important that a leader check in with James to see how he is affected by what just transpired. While SusAnne says her shoulders feel lighter, James makes what appear to be out-of-awareness movements with his shoulders, sending a nonverbal message that he is feeling burdened. In this role play with SusAnne, James taps into his own feelings over a previous relationship with a woman in his life. The role play between SusAnne and James is another example of maximizing transference reactions and getting two people engaged in therapeutic work. As a result of the reciprocal exchange, both SusAnne and James have a sense of relief. SusAnne notes how much better it feels to her when she even temporarily lets go of these painful feelings. She makes a decision that she does not have to keep her feelings bottled up. She is also more open to relationships with other people in her life without too quickly assuming that they are not to be trusted and that they will hurt her. Furthermore, SusAnne can continue to remind herself how freeing it is when she refuses to accept all the responsibility for what went wrong in her prior relationship. James becomes aware of how important it is to him to have been forgiven in this symbolic role play. Although he realizes that his girlfriend may not be as forgiving, he wants to be able to forgive himself.

---

[17] For a discussion of utilizing techniques in dealing with a member's metaphors, see *Group Techniques* (Chapter 1).

At the end of the dialogue between SusAnne and James, he initiates a hug. When James asks the coleaders for permission, we tell him that he needs to check this out with SusAnne. He does and SusAnne is able to respond. However, had James asked SusAnne for a hug prematurely, when she was expressing her anger and hurt toward him, we would have intervened to curtail his attempts to dissipate the intensity of her feelings. Physical contact among members is often therapeutic, but it should not be allowed to short-circuit a member's expression and exploration of his or her pain.

We pay attention to the nonverbal communication of members, believing that these signals are often more important than what is being said. We look for patterns of nonverbal communication but avoid quickly interpreting the meaning underlying these messages. Instead, we ask clients to become aware of their own body and other nonverbal forms of communication and attach their own meanings to what they are expressing bodily. This is particularly illustrated in the exchange between SusAnne and James.

1. How were you personally affected as you observed SusAnne's work? How might this influence your work with her?

_____

_____

_____

2. If some of your own unfinished business and pain over a relationship were tapped, would you disclose this to the group? Why or why not? If you disclosed your reactions, how might this facilitate or hinder your work with SusAnne and James?

_____

_____

_____

3. In the video, SusAnne symbolically gives back to her boyfriend the hurt, shame, and lies she has been carrying around. What therapeutic purpose, if any, do you see in this technique?

_____

_____

_____

Andrew's Struggle of Keeping Pain Inside

VIEW VIDEO SECTION 25: ANDREW'S STRUGGLE OF KEEPING PAIN INSIDE

Marianne and Jerry know that Andrew has also talked about his painful divorce, and it is likely that he has been very affected by what transpired between SusAnne and James. But Andrew does not express what he is feeling. Operating on a hunch, Jerry asks Andrew how he was affected. Indeed, Andrew acknowledges that this interchange brought up his pain over his previous relationship. Jerry asks Andrew to look at and tell SusAnne about how he has been hurt and how he shuts people out. He declines at first, stating that he does not want to get back to that pain. As he puts it, "I want to let my hurt go out the back door. I want to put it in the freezer." However, he does continue to talk about his pain, while staying quite cognitive. He describes his pain graphically as "It's like I've been stabbed." Jerry asks, "Where?" Andrew replies, "In my core. In my soul and heart. My very sensitive part." It is clear that Andrew labors and is ambivalent over making himself vulnerable with people versus shutting them out and keeping them isolated. Only a small segment of the interchanges with Andrew is seen in the video as his exploration is slow and tedious.

At one point Marianne asks him, "Do you see any hope for yourself?" He replies, "I see a lot of hope. It's just if I will take that key and open the door. I want to open the door a little bit." Marianne asks Andrew how he can let us in a little bit right now in this room. He does not respond to her invitation. Marianne also asks him, "What can you do to avoid being disappointed by the end of the group?" He thinks about this for a while. Then Marianne teases him, "You sure think a lot. You wear me out! Do you realize how hard I am working with you?" Both Marianne and Andrew laugh. This kind of humor must be timely and should be based on a trusting relationship. Humor must never be at the client's expense, nor should it be aimed at putting down or embarrassing the client. We tend to use humor as therapeutic leverage, which often helps members put into perspective the meaning they ascribe to a situation.

There is another noteworthy aspect of Andrew's struggle. Andrew comments several times that he isolates and is not able to reach out to people. Yet he was given feedback by both the leaders and some members that he had an inclination to be supportive toward a particular member at different junctures during the group, but he stopped himself. For example, when Casey cried, Andrew sat next to her and wanted to reach out to her, yet he stopped himself, which was a pattern for him. It is important that he hears the feedback that it is not true that he is unable to feel for others, but that he holds himself back from doing what he is inclined to do. Therefore, the focus is not to get Andrew to feel, but to get him to express more readily those feelings that do emerge within him. Making himself vulnerable in this way is still a scary step for him to take. At least at this time in his life, he is not sure how much he wants to open himself to others.

At a later session, Andrew and Jerry engage in a role-playing situation. Andrew gives voice to his emotional and soft side, while Jerry plays the defiant and critical side. When Andrew seems ready to shift, he then plays the hard and critical side of himself, and Jerry assumes the gentle and caring side of Andrew. This technique is an illustration of externalizing an internal debate that often goes on within Andrew. At times, we direct members to express out loud what appear to be conflicting sides of themselves. We ask them to stay with one side for some time, and exaggerate that side. Doing so, they are often in a position to decide how they might want to integrate these sides more harmoniously into their personality. Andrew learns that he does not need to live exclusively by one side of himself. As he put it, "There are two parts of me. I would like to mate my gentle and caring side with the fearless and defiant side."

The therapeutic intervention with Andrew's struggle illustrates dealing with polarities. Many of the techniques we use involve the exploration of polarities in members, even though members may not want to acknowledge what seem like opposite sides within them (such as a tender side and a tough side). We may ask members to exaggerate one side of themselves a bit longer to get more information about that side and to decide whether it is a way they want to be. These techniques are not aimed at getting rid of one of these aspects of self but at helping the member acknowledge a part that may be neglected or rejected.[18]

1. What is your reaction as you observe and listen to Andrew's pain over his divorce? How might your reactions affect your ability to work with him?

_____

_____

2. Andrew says, "I want to let my hurt go out the back door. I want to put it in the freezer." How might you intervene?

_____

_____

3. How accepting are you of what Andrew accomplished in the group? Explain.

_____

_____

_____

[18] For a discussion of utilizing techniques in dealing with the theme, "A part of me wants this, and a part of me wants that," see *Group Techniques* (Chapter 6).

COREYS' COMMENTARY: THE WORKING STAGE

As usual, at the end of this day we ask members to participate in a check-out. They make a few remarks about what this day was like for them, how they felt about what they did, and what they are learning from their exploration.

During the sessions you just saw, one member (Casey) comes forth and declares she is ready to do some of the work she came here to do. Much of what followed demonstrates the impact Casey had on other members and how they tapped into their unfinished business with their parents. Even though some of these members did not declare parental issues as a part of their initial agenda, they were drawn into feelings about their parents at this juncture. We often see this occurring in groups, and we sometimes mention to members to be prepared to deal with issues that spontaneously emerge.

Many members became intensively emotional as they talked about their painful experiences as children. This is not uncommon, especially during the working stage of a cohesive group. The emotionality of one member often sparks the emotions of others. However, a group can be productive and meaningful to members even if a great deal of emotional expression is not present. We do not want to set up the expectation or establish a norm that for a group to be productive everybody has to cry or experience a catharsis. In some groups there is little expression of intense emotions, yet the group is functioning well and achieving its goals. The interactions may focus on more subtle and seemingly less dramatic issues, but the key point is that the group is characterized by a willingness to work through material rather than a tendency to shelve issues.

SUMMARY OF THE WORKING STAGE

Basic Characteristics of the Working Stage. How many of the points listed below did you observe in the group session? When a group reaches the working stage, the central characteristics include the following:

- The level of trust and cohesion is high.
- Communication within the group is open and involves an accurate expression of what is being experienced.
- Members interact with one another freely and directly.
- There is a willingness to risk threatening material and to make oneself known to others; members bring to the group personal topics they want to discuss and understand better.
- Conflict among members is recognized and dealt with directly and effectively.
- Feedback is given freely and accepted and considered nondefensively.
- Confrontation occurs in a way in which those doing the challenging avoid judgmental labeling of others.
- Members are willing to work outside the group to achieve behavioral changes.
- Participants feel supported in their attempts to change and are willing to risk new behavior.
- Members feel hopeful that they can change if they are willing to take action; they do not feel helpless.

Member Functions. The working stage is characterized by the exploration of personally meaningful material. What did you observe in the group? To reach a working stage, members have the following tasks:

- Initiating topics they want to explore
- Giving others feedback and being open to receiving it
- Sharing how they are affected by others' presence and work in the group
- Practicing new skills and behaviors in daily life and bringing the results to the sessions
- Offering both challenge and support to others and engaging in self-confrontation
- Continually assessing their satisfaction with the group and actively taking steps to change their level of involvement in the sessions if necessary

Leader Functions. What leader interventions and functions did you observe in the group? Some of the central leadership functions at this stage include the following:

- Providing systematic reinforcement of desired group behaviors that foster cohesion and productive work
- Looking for common themes among members' work that provide for some universality
- Continuing to model appropriate behavior, especially caring confrontation, and disclosing ongoing reactions to the group
- Supporting members' willingness to take risks and assisting them in carrying this behavior into their daily living
- Interpreting the meaning of behavior patterns at appropriate times so members can reach a deeper level of self-exploration and consider alternative behaviors
- Focusing on the importance of translating insight into action
- Encouraging members to keep in mind what they want from the group and to ask for it[19]

QUESTIONS FOR APPLYING THE SUMMARY LIST

Now that you have watched this segment of the group during its working stage, apply the above summary list to the following questions concerning the group.

1. What theoretical framework did you see the coleaders drawing from during this session?

_____

_____

_____

2. What is one technique that you found to be most interesting?

_____

_____

_____

3. During the working stage of this group, what do you see as your main function as a group leader?

_____

_____

_____

4. What value do you see in linking the work of several members?

_____

_____

_____

IN-CLASS EXERCISE: QUESTIONS FOR SMALL GROUP DISCUSSION AND REFLECTING TEAMS

Form reflecting teams in small groups within your class. After viewing the working stage of this group, share your observations and reactions. In your small group, focus on what you heard and saw

---

[19] For a discussion of moving from the transition to the working stage, characteristics of the working stage, therapeutic factors operating in a group, and member and leader functions at the working stage, see *Groups: Process and Practice* (Chapter 8). For a description of techniques for exploring material and emerging themes for the working stage, see *Group Techniques* (Chapter 6). For a summary of issues pertaining to the working stage of a group's development, see *Theory and Practice of Group Counseling* (Chapter 5, text and student manual). For a discussion of applying different theoretical perspectives in working with themes emerging from the group, see *Theory and Practice of Group Counseling* (Chapter 17, text and student manual).

and on the interactions that stood out for you during the working stage of this group. Pay particular attention to how you are personally affected by the members and the leaders and how that might influence the way you would lead this group.

1. From what you observed from the video during this phase of group, how ready are you to deal with intense feelings that members might bring out in a group?

2. What value do you see in the expression of emotions in a group?

3. To what degree have you identified in your own life some of the personal issues that the members brought out in the video? To what extent have you explored some of these issues?

4. What do you look for in a group to assess the degree to which that group is engaged in productive work?

5. What are some of the main lessons you are learning about how to best facilitate interaction among the participants in a group?

6. What would you have learned about yourself had you been a member of a group such as this one? If you had been a leader?

7. What ethical issues can you raise concerning this segment of the group?

Part V: The Ending Stage

Directions: Complete this brief self-inventory before viewing the ending stage of the group. The purpose of the self-inventory is to help you identify and clarify your attitudes and beliefs about the variety of group process concepts, techniques, and issues in group leadership. The statements on the inventory are not simply right or wrong, true or false. Decide the degree to which you agree or disagree with these statements. Then, after viewing this segment, look over your responses to see whether you want to modify them in any way. This self-inventory will help you express your views and think about the ideas you'll encounter in this section.

Using the following code, write next to each statement the number of the response that most closely reflects your viewpoint:

5 = I *strongly agree* with this statement.
4 = I *agree*, in most respects, with this statement.
3 = I am *undecided* in my opinion about this statement.
2 = I *disagree*, in most respects, with this statement.
1 = I *strongly disagree* with this statement.

_____ 1. I am very much in favor of asking members to evaluate the impact of the group experience at the last meeting.

_____ 2. I am inclined to use structured exercises to assist members in consolidating their learning.

_____ 3. I would structure some final sessions so that each member both gives and receives feedback.

_____ 4. Scheduling a follow-up meeting seems like a way to soften the difficulties involved in making a separation.

_____ 5. If the group members worked successfully, then conflict would certainly be absent at the ending sessions.

_____ 6. I would have a difficult time saying good-bye if I had become close to the members in a group I was leading.

_____ 7. It is a good idea to ask members to formulate a contract that specifies how they are likely to carry out their learning in daily life once the group ends.

_____ 8. Before the final meeting I would bring up the topics of potentially reverting to old patterns and the tendency to discount what one has learned.

Reflecting on Afterthoughts

VIEW VIDEO SECTION 26: REFLECTING ON AFTERTHOUGHTS

We open the last day of the group by reminding the members that this is a day for reflecting on what they have accomplished and for spending time talking about how they might carry their new learning into their everyday lives. We mention the importance of writing in their journal as a way of keeping track of what they learned, what steps they took in this group to bring about change, and what they want to apply to everyday life. Jerry asks the members if they have any afterthoughts about the work they did the previous day, because if they do, this needs to be brought out and dealt with at least briefly.

From experience, we know that members sometimes have residual feelings about intense emotional work at a subsequent session, and they frequently have new insights associated with their work. Marianne asks the members if they have any regrets about what they did or did not do in an earlier session, or any reactions to other members. It is important to structure sessions during the ending phase that will allow time for exploration of any residual feelings.

Preparing Members for Termination

VIEW VIDEO SECTION 27: PREPARING MEMBERS FOR TERMINATION

At this ending stage, our task as coleaders is to prepare members for termination. It is important to remind members about the limited time left so that they can bring closure to the group experience. We give members adequate time to share and work through their feelings and thoughts about termination of the group. It is essential that they identify any unfinished business pertaining to the group in advance of the final group session. We tell members that the last meeting is neither the time to introduce new work, nor is it the time to bring up reactions to others that they have kept to themselves for the course of the entire group. Here are some questions we ask members as the group moves toward termination:

- What were a few of the turning points in this group for you?
- What most stands out for you about being in this group?
- What is it like for you to realize that this group will end?
- What would you like to take away from this group and use in your life?
- What contracts do you want to make?
- How you can use others in the group as a source of support?

1. How do you deal with endings in your personal life? How might that influence the manner in which you address group endings?

_____

_____

_____

2. What are your ethical responsibilities to group members at the termination of their group? Explain.

_____

_____

_____

Consolidating Learning

Some specific statements about the group by members, along with a brief comment on our part, follow:

DARREN: I feel so much better now.

(Remembering that Darren stated earlier his concerns about being perceived as weak if he were to cry, Jerry asks him if he has any thoughts or feelings about the time in group that he cried and expressed some painful childhood memories. Darren is not critical of expressing his emotions and adds that what helped him was to check out the group after he completed an intense piece of work earlier. We also challenge Darren and others who may have a tendency to be critical of what they said or did in a group to consider what they might do when they no longer have the support of the group. Although Darren talks about his reactions to expressing himself emotionally and eventually feels better about doing this, later he may begin to experience doubts and wonder if what he did was "weak." If Darren is self-critical of showing emotion, it would be useful for him to practice talking back to the critical inner voices during a group session, and then continue to practice challenging his negative self-talk outside the group.)

JACKIE: I realize that I am not so boring, and I'm not as critical of myself. Now I see that some areas where I was the most critical are really my assets. Now I'm able to feel nurturing from you.

(We want to know what it is like for her to allow herself to receive nurturance from others because this is a shift for her. We also ask her what she did that resulted in her being more accepting of herself.)

ANDREW: The cognitive role play that I did helped me see that there are both soft and hard sides of me.

(We challenge Andrew to continue reflecting on which side of himself he wants to express more frequently. We ask him to consider the emotional price of keeping people out and remaining emotionally tough.)

SusAnne explored some issues pertaining to her mother (not shown on the video), as well as her former boyfriend. She has more clarity on what she would want to say to her mom, and she would like to be able to initiate a different kind of dialogue with her. At this juncture, we could give SusAnne an opportunity to engage in a brief behavioral rehearsal where she picks a mom from the group and makes a few key statements that she wants her mom to really hear. We need to let members like SusAnne know that this is not the time for extensive exploration, but more for identifying a few specific things she might say in a future discussion with her mother.

Dealing With Unexpected Conflict

VIEW VIDEO SECTION 28: DEALING WITH UNEXPECTED CONFLICT

Although conflict most often manifests itself during the transition stage, conflict can occur at any time in the life of a group. Dealing with conflict is not something that is settled once and for all. At the final session, James alludes to a conflict that occurred out of group prior to this last meeting, and he wonders how people are reacting to him. He quickly wants to sidestep any discussion of the conflict, indicating that maybe later we could talk.

Sensing that there is something in the group that is not being said, Marianne says to James, "Later may be now." She realizes that if the conflict is not addressed, the other pressing business during the ending phase is not likely to be dealt with effectively. The conflict between James and several other members, which occurred outside of the group the night before, was talked about and resolved in this last group session. Misunderstandings were cleared up through dialogue. It didn't take long to address this unfinished business, but it was critical that it was not bypassed.

1. As a leader, how will you deal with a conflict that does not surface until the end of a group?

_____

_____

_____

2. What might you do if members did not seem to be able to resolve a conflict situation during the final session of a group?

_____

_____

_____

Keeping Members Focused

VIEW VIDEO SECTION 29: KEEPING MEMBERS FOCUSED

Marianne announces that we have a different agenda today, meaning that we will be focusing on helping members consolidate their learning. Marianne says, "We would like for each of you to identify one specific thing that you might carry out of this group into your lives." It is the task of the coleaders at this time to keep members focused and to give all the members a chance to zero in on specific lessons they've learned. Although only a few members' comments are shown in the video, typically we structure an ending session in such a manner that everyone has roughly equal time and that nobody is left out. During both the initial and final sessions, we want to hear all the members' voices.

Another focusing question that we typically raise toward the end of a group is, "Do any of you have any different perceptions now than you did when you first joined this group?" Some of the members responded in the following ways:

JYL: I put myself out there and took risks.

DARREN: I see the humanness as I look around this group.

ANDREW: I don't see the masks on people now.

JACKIE: I feel seen and still loved.

CASEY: I'm not rehearsing, and my head doesn't hurt. I'm remembering how afraid I was and how I feel differently now.

JACQUELINE: I'm feeling approved of. Mother is not here in the form of any of you.

1. A member says, "I don't want this group to end. I'd like to see us continue meeting as a group." What would you be inclined to do?

_____

_____

_____

2. What would you say to the members of your group about dealing with setbacks once they leave the group?

_____

_____

_____

Noticing Changes and Taking Credit for Them

We encourage members to reflect on what they did in group and how that contributed to what they learned. Once members specify ways they behaved differently, they are in a better position to implement this learning in future situations. We also ask members to reflect on how their life might be different if they were to function to their full potential. As one of the members initiates the holding of hands as a closure experience, Marianne asks everyone to look around the room and notice any differences from when the group first convened. Generally, there is a greater sense of cohesion in the group, and members feel more connected to others because of the nature of the risks that were taken. There is more identification with one another because of the willingness of members to reveal sensitive personal aspects of themselves. The room does indeed feel different. Marianne says, "I hope you remember, not only that you are feeling good and close to one another, but that you remember how you made this happen."

COREYS' COMMENTARY: THE ENDING STAGE

Much of the focus of this session is on bringing closure to what members did during the weekend. Our central focus is now on assisting members in consolidating their learning. What you see on the video regarding termination issues is a very small part of what actually occurred in the group. As a group evolves toward termination, we explore a number of tasks, including feelings of separation, unfinished business, reviewing the group experience, practicing for behavioral change, giving and receiving feedback, talking about ways to carry their learning into daily life, making contracts of what to do after a group ends, and talking about a follow-up meeting. We remind members again about the importance of maintaining confidentiality. We also ask members to talk about what they might do to discount what they actually did during the group, how they might recover from setbacks, and how to create support systems.

We sincerely hope this self-study program has been a useful and enjoyable process for you. We hope you will find ways to continue learning about groups and practicing leadership skills. The single most important element in effective group leadership is your way of being in a group. In the video you saw us utilize a variety of techniques in dealing with the themes members introduced. These techniques were used as means to further the agenda presented to us by members, not as ends in themselves. Techniques are merely tools to amplify emerging material and to encourage exploration of issues that have personal relevance to members. Techniques are not useful if they are not sensitively adapted to the particular client and context. The outcome of a technique is affected by the climate of the group and by the relationship between the coleaders and the members.

More important than the techniques we use are the attitudes we have toward members, which are manifested by who we are and what we do in the group. When we are fully present and ourselves, we can be a catalyst for members to engage in introspection, relevant self-disclosure, and risk-taking. Sometimes group participants show us their worst, and we are privileged to be part of their journey as they discover their best. We believe that our primary function as coleaders is to support members in their journey of making decisions regarding how they want to live. We work with people who are often struggling and who are experiencing psychological pain. The group experience affords members avenues for living more peacefully with themselves and with others.

SUMMARY OF THE ENDING STAGE

Basic Characteristics of the Ending Stage. During the ending stage of a group, the following characteristics are typically evident:

- Members may pull back and participate in less intense ways, in anticipation of the ending of the group.
- Members may express different feelings over the ending of a group as well as fears about being able to implement what they learned in the group.
- Members are encouraged to evaluate the group experience.
- Discussion about follow-up meetings or some plan for accountability will encourage members to carry out their plans for change.

Member Functions. The major task facing members during the final stage of a group is consolidating their learning and transferring what they have learned to their outside environment. Of course, they have been doing this to some extent between sessions if the group has been meeting on a weekly basis. This is the time for members to review the process and outcomes of the entire group and put into some cognitive framework the meaning of the group experience. Some tasks for members at this time are to:

- Deal with their feelings about separation and termination
- Prepare for generalizing their learning to everyday situations
- Give others a better picture of how they are perceived
- Complete any unfinished business concerning either issues they have brought into the group or issues that pertain to people in the group
- Evaluate the impact of the group
- Make decisions and plans concerning what changes they want to make and how they will go about making them

Leader Functions. The group leader's central tasks in the consolidation phase are to provide a structure that helps participants clarify the meaning of their experiences in the group and to assist members in generalizing their learning from the group to everyday situations. Tasks at this period include:

- Assisting members in dealing with any feelings they may have about termination
- Giving members an opportunity to express and deal with any unfinished business within the group
- Reinforcing changes that members have made and ensuring that members have information about resources to enable them to make further changes
- Assisting members in determining how they will apply specific skills in a variety of situations in daily life
- Working with members to develop specific contracts and homework assignments as practical ways of making changes
- Assisting participants to develop a conceptual framework that will help them understand, integrate, consolidate, and remember what they have learned in the group

- Providing opportunities for members to give one another constructive feedback
- Reemphasizing the importance of maintaining confidentiality after the group ends[20]

QUESTIONS FOR APPLYING THE SUMMARY LIST

Now that you have watched this segment of the group during its ending stage, apply the above summary list to the following questions concerning the group.

1. What do you consider your main leadership function to be at the ending stage of a group?

_____

_____

_____

2. What are some of the questions the leaders asked of the members that you found most helpful?

_____

_____

_____

3. What are the *main challenges* you expect to face as your group moves toward termination?

_____

_____

_____

IN-CLASS EXERCISE: QUESTIONS FOR SMALL GROUP DISCUSSION AND REFLECTING TEAMS

Form reflecting teams in small groups within your class. After viewing the final stage of this group, share your observations and reactions. In your small group, focus on what you heard and saw, on the interactions that stood out for you, and the most salient moments during the final stage of this group.

1. How would you prepare members for the termination phase of a group?
2. What difficulties, if any, do you expect to encounter during the ending phase of a group? For yourself from a personal perspective? From the group members?
3. How inclined would you be to arrange a follow-up session for the group?
4. What are some ways you would evaluate the outcomes of your group?
5. What techniques would be most useful during the final stage of a group?
6. What ethical issues are most relevant during the final stage of a group?

---

[20] For a discussion of issues pertaining to the termination of a group experience, characteristics of the ending stage, member and leader functions, and follow-up approaches, see *Groups: Process and Practice* (Chapter 9). For a discussion of techniques for terminating a group, see *Group Techniques* (Chapter 7). For a summary of issues pertaining to the later stages of a group's development, see *Theory and Practice of Group Counseling* (Chapter 5, text and student manual). For a discussion of applying different theoretical perspectives in working with themes emerging from the group, see *Theory and Practice of Group Counseling* (Chapter 17, text and student manual).

Part VI: Ethical Issues in the Practice of Group Counseling

A mark of professional group leadership is establishing a set of guiding principles. In this section we present some ethical guidelines that are relevant to what you observed in the group and in the workbook discussion of procedures used to facilitate this group. We hope these guidelines stimulate your thinking about ways to ensure ethical practice.

1. It is essential to have a clear idea of what your roles and functions are in the group so you can communicate them to the members.
2. Have a clear idea of the type of group you are designing.
3. Develop a means of screening that will allow you to differentiate between suitable and unsuitable applicants.
4. Consider the advantages of having some kind of pregroup meeting to orient members to a group.
5. Tell prospective group members what is expected of them.
6. Make prospective participants aware of the techniques that will be employed and of the exercises that they may be asked to participate in.
7. Avoid undertaking a project beyond the scope of your training and experience.
8. Make clear at the outset of a group what the focus will be.
9. Protect the members' right to decide what to share with the group and what activities to participate in.
10. Develop a rationale for using group interventions, and be able to verbalize it.
11. Be thoroughly grounded in a number of diverse theoretical orientations as a basis for creating your own personalized style of leading groups.
12. Be aware of the cultural context as you work with members.
13. Be willing to discuss with members the psychological risks involved in group participation both before they enter and also when it is appropriate throughout the life of the group.
14. Emphasize the importance of confidentiality to members before they enter a group, during the group sessions when relevant, and before the group terminates.
15. When it is appropriate, be open with the group about your values, but avoid imposing them on clients.
16. Make referral resources available to people who need or desire further psychological assistance.
17. Encourage participants to discuss their experience in the group and help them evaluate the degree to which they are meeting their personal goals.
18. Assist members in applying what they have learned in the group situation to life outside of group and prepare them for possible setbacks.
19. Schedule a follow-up session so members are able to see how others in their group have done and so you have a basis for evaluating the impact of the group experience.
20. Develop some method of evaluation to determine the effectiveness of your interventions in the group.

Go over the ethical guidelines above and circle the numbers of items that you consider to be particularly important. Do you have additional ethical concerns not mentioned above in thinking about leading a group?

_____

_____

_____

_____

_____

_____

Part VII: Follow-Up Self-Inventory

Now that you have worked through all the stages in the evolution of this group in conjunction with the workbook, we suggest that you take this inventory to determine how any of your perspectives on group process may have changed. Use the following code:

5 = I *strongly agree* with1 this statement.
4 = I *agree*, in most respects, with this statement.
3 = I am *undecided* in my opinion about this statement.
2 = I *disagree*, in most respects, with this statement.
1 = I *strongly disagree* with this statement.

_____ 1. To create a sense of trust among the members, I would be inclined to ask members to talk about any reservations they have pertaining to the safety of the room.

_____ 2. Confidentiality needs to be taught to group members and monitored during the life of a group.

_____ 3. Early in the course of a group, one of my main tasks is to assist members in formulating specific personal goals.

_____ 4. If I become emotionally involved in a group as the leader, then I lose my objectivity, which restricts my effectiveness.

_____ 5. I see it as essential that I am willing to engage in appropriate self-disclosure, even though I am facilitating the group.

_____ 6. I prefer coleading a group to leading alone.

_____ 7. Resistance in a member or in the group as a whole is generally due to inept group leadership.

_____ 8. Conflict among or between members and leaders is usually a destructive element indicating that cohesion is absent within the group.

_____ 9. If members express fears related to participating in the group, it is generally a good idea for others to quickly provide a great deal of reassurance.

_____ 10. There are clear demarcations between each of the stages of a group.

_____ 11. Leader confrontation of members should be avoided at all costs until the group has reached a working stage.

_____ 12. A sign of a working stage is a willingness on the part of members to spontaneously involve themselves in interactions within the group.

_____ 13. If my group does not reach a working stage, this is a sign that very little learning has taken place.

_____ 14. Unless most of the members of a group have expressed intense emotions, it can hardly be said that this group has achieved a working stage.

_____ 15. Linking one member to another member and asking each of them to talk directly to each other typically is unproductive.

_____ 16. Facilitating members to focus on their awareness of here-and-now reactions is a useful way to create a trusting climate.

_____ 17. Once the group reaches a working stage, group leaders are really not necessary.

_____ 18. Members can frequently create an agenda for their personal work in a group by paying attention to how others affect them and sharing their reactions with others.

_____ 19. The use of contracts is an effective way of helping members put an action plan into operation outside of the group.

_____ 20. It is important to give members an opportunity to deal with unfinished business within the group toward the ending phase.

_____ 21. I would structure some final sessions so that each member both gives and receives feedback.

_____ 22. In designing techniques for group facilitation, it is essential to consider the client's cultural background.

_____ 23. Any indication of leader countertransference is a clear indication that he or she is unable to effectively lead a group.

_____ 24. The most important aspect of being a competent group leader is the ability to apply leadership skills.

_____ 25. The group leader's willingness to use him- or herself as a therapeutic instrument is of the utmost importance.

Go over this inventory and circle the numbers of items where you think the greatest degree of learning has occurred. Which items most stood out for you in this list, and why?

_____

_____

_____

_____

_____

_____

_____

Part VIII: Some Final Thoughts

As you participated in this self-study on group process, we hope you were able to appreciate that group facilitation involves far more than applying techniques or solving problems. As you have seen, being in a group is a personal experience for both the members and the coleaders.

The video you watched and studied is a unique educational endeavor because the group members are being themselves, rather than enacting a predetermined script. It is difficult to watch this video in a purely objective and detached fashion. As you watched sections of this video, you may have become personally involved because the participants were exploring universal themes that connect us in the human condition. When you work with clients, you will most likely be affected by certain problems they bring up or with emotions they express. If you were affected personally as you reviewed the video, take this opportunity to seek some therapeutic paths to explore your own feelings and thoughts.

WHERE ARE YOU NOW AND WHERE WILL YOU GO FROM HERE?

As a final exercise, we ask you to reflect on your significant learnings from viewing the video and completing the workbook and to clarify where you want to go from here.

1. How has your view of group counseling changed after viewing this first program (*Evolution of a Group*) and completing the activities in this workbook?

_____

_____

_____

_____

_____

_____

_____

_____

2. What are some of your major learnings regarding how to become an effective group member? Group leader?

_____

_____

_____

_____

_____

_____

_____

_____

_____

3. What are some major things you learned about yourself as a person, and how is this likely to influence your work as a group counselor?

_____

_____

_____

_____

_____

_____

_____

_____

4. What are some questions that viewing the video and completing the workbook have raised for you?

_____

_____

_____

_____

_____

_____

_____

5. Where will you go from here as you work toward your development as an effective group counselor?

_____

_____

_____

_____

_____

_____

_____

_____

SECOND PROGRAM:

Challenges Facing Group Leaders

Part I: Overview

HOW AND WHY THIS SECOND PROGRAM ORIGINATED

Both professionals and students in our group counseling workshops and courses tell us that dealing with problematic behaviors exhibited by group members is the major challenge they face. In our teaching we have been attempting to reframe resistance because it generally carries negative connotations toward group members. *Challenges Facing Group Leaders* demonstrates ways of reframing resistance and provides examples of how to work therapeutically with defensive behaviors exhibited by group members. Because of the interest we have found in addressing difficult situations that group leaders encounter, we decided that an ideal follow-up to the first program (*Evolution of a Group*) would be to focus on ways of thinking about and dealing with a variety of challenges in groups. This second program consists of the following vignettes, which were enacted through role playing to simulate working through some of the difficult issues that are of great interest to group practitioners.

1. Checking in: What was it like to return to group?
2. The leaders let me down.
3. I'm not feeling safe in here.
4. I didn't want to come back to group.
5. I'm in this group against my will.
6. Emotions make me uncomfortable.
7. I'm self-conscious about my accent.
8. I want the leaders to disclose more.
9. I learn a lot by being quiet.
10. Silence serves a function.
11. I feel pressured to disclose.
12. What's wrong with helping others?
13. Can't we stop all this conflict?
14. I feel weak when I show feelings.
15. Checking out: What is each of you taking from this session?
16. What does my culture have to do with my identity?
17. I feel different from others in here.
18. Sometimes I want to exclude others.
19. I struggle with language.
20. I resent being stereotyped.
21. We are alike and we are different.
22. I express myself better in my native language.
23. I am colorblind.
24. I know little about my culture.
25. I want more answers from you leaders.

We identified the above themes through a survey of colleagues who teach group counseling courses. The topics receiving the highest ratings were chosen as the focus for creating a variety of scenarios. Our work with students also helped us select the topics chosen for this program. Part 2 of this program explores the "challenges of dealing with difficult behaviors in groups." Part 3 examines "the challenges of addressing diversity issues."

ABOUT THIS SECOND PROGRAM

In *Challenges Facing Group Leaders* the emphasis is on the part of the process of a group that tends to create the most anxiety and concern for group practitioners—the early stages of a group's development. In the first program, you observed and studied a group progressing through all the stages from the beginning to the end. In contrast, this second program deals with a more limited perspective by focusing on the challenges at the initial and transition stages. The scenarios that you see in the *Challenges* program can occur at any stage in a group, but the themes enacted primarily occur during the early phases of a group. Our central aim is to address ways of encouraging members to explore concerns they have about their experience in a group. If the key tasks of the early stage of a group are not adequately attended to, then the safety in that group is inhibited. For a group to achieve the trust necessary to engage in productive work, it is essential that concerns of members be identified and addressed. Leaders sometimes find the foundational work demonstrated in this program to be tedious and slow, and some may want to quickly get down to doing "real work." The themes that are portrayed illustrate ways to therapeutically deal with potential problems and with lack of cooperation on the part of members. For example, if members feel they are being stereotyped within the group, it is critical that they are given opportunities to express and work through their thoughts and feelings. If this process is short-circuited, then a weak foundation is built that does not allow significant work to occur at a later stage in the group.

Although the scenarios you see in this program are essentially role-played, the group members drew from their own personal issues and experiences from group counseling to enact the scenarios. To help you better understand what we asked each group participant in the *Challenges* program to do, here is an excerpt from the written guidelines we gave to each of the group members in the program:

How can you best prepare yourself psychologically for this project? Although we will not be filming a "real" group documentary such as the one you saw in *Evolution of a Group*, we hope you will be yourself as much as possible (even though you will be enacting different roles). Each of you has taken a group counseling course and has had experiences as a group member, has participated in training workshops for group leaders, and has coled several groups. As you think about the scenarios for the program, put yourself in each scenario by thinking about situations that have been challenging for you both as a member and as a coleader. We ask you to draw upon your experiences in groups. Give some reflection on these questions as a way to get ready for the filming:

1. Do you remember what it was like for you when you first were in a group?

2. Do you recall what you felt when you coled your first group?

3. How motivated were you to participate? How much did you challenge yourself?

4. In what ways might you have been reluctant or cautious as a member?

5. When you led a group, can you remember the particular group members you perceived to be the most difficult? How did these members affect you personally and your ability to function in the group?

6. What were some of the most difficult and challenging situations you encountered as a member? As a group facilitator? How did you address these challenges?

As is the case with any group we conduct, we emphasize ethical aspects, such as informed consent. The group participants selected for this second program were thoroughly prepared through letters explaining the nature of the proposed educational program. Many telephone conversations and e-mail exchanges with each of them helped clarify what we were attempting to accomplish in this project: the specific purposes of this program, the content of the program, and what would be expected of them. Even though the members were expected to role-play a variety of scenarios illustrating problematic situations in a group, we also encouraged them to draw on their personal experiences in groups as a way to make the enactments as real as possible. There was no script and no rehearsals. This weekend group was a blend of role playing specific scenarios and genuine interactions within the group context. The program consists primarily of the participants enacting problematic behaviors, but assuming a particular role sometimes evoked some very real reactions.

OUR EXPERIENCE AS COLEADERS

Designing this group and coleading it proved especially challenging. In some ways, it was more difficult to switch from one theme to another and to enact problematic situations than to conduct a group from beginning to end. We wanted to be sensitive when members found themselves triggered in personal ways during the filming, and when members did express their feelings about life experiences we did not abruptly move on from scenario to scenario. This resulted in many more hours of film than we could use in a 90-minute program. We did our best to be ourselves and to colead in a fashion that is typical of us in any group we facilitate. The interventions you see in this filmed group are very much like the ones we often make. For example, when members confronted us through a role-playing situation, we addressed this as though it were an authentic situation. By giving ourselves the latitude to respond "as if" the situations enacted were reality, we did not have to "act." We are not attempting to demonstrate the "one right way" to intervene in a problem situation; there are many appropriate responses leaders might make to the same situation. Our intention is to generate thought regarding how you might intervene in similar situations to those you will view in the program.

We frequently asked members if they were willing to work more fully on a given issue that was identified in the scenarios filmed, but this work was not included in this program. You see much more of this work in the first video program (*Evolution of a Group*) as we illustrate our work with several members at the different stages of a group. However, by using the workbook you can get a sense of the direction in which we might proceed with members in our collaborative efforts to include them in ways to bring about change. For instance, a member might say, "I would like to feel that I have more of a voice in this group, and I hope I will feel freer in speaking up." In the Group Leaders' Reflections section in the workbook, we provide additional information about specific ways we assisted participants in clarifying what they wanted and how they could best get this in the group setting.

THE SEATING ARRANGEMENT
You will notice that the group is sitting in a horseshoe configuration. This was done for the purposes of filming and is not the way we typically arrange a group. Members decide where they will sit at each session, and as coleaders we generally sit across from each other.

HOW TO USE THE VIDEO AND THE WORKBOOK
It is essential to use the workbook in conjunction with this second program. The video presents brief scenarios, which are elaborated upon in the workbook.

We suggest that you initially view this second program in its entirety to get a general sense of the action within the group sessions. After doing this, view the program again section by section. Each section is numbered with a subtitle (and a number) on the screen. After you view each of these sections illustrating a particular scenario, stop the video and go to this workbook. We suggest you read the Key Points of the Group Session as a way to focus on the main elements in the enactment of the scenario you just viewed. This is followed by a Your Reflections and Responses section designed to bring you into the program in an interactive manner. Write your responses to the questions we pose. After doing this, read our commentary, Group Leaders' Reflections. Here we talk out loud about what we were thinking in the segment you just watched. We describe what we see as going on, give a brief explanation about why we intervened as we did, and say a few words about where we might pursue work with different members. By taking the time to pause the video, reflect on what you just observed, write your reactions, and read our account of the scenario, you will become actively engaged in this interactive program.

Part II: Challenges of Dealing With Difficult Behaviors in Group

For those who lead groups, numerous challenges invariably arise. Human diversity and the many behaviors that participants express in the group setting demonstrate the complexity of this process for leaders.

INTRODUCTORY COMMENTARY

Key Points in the Commentary

- Viewers will see role plays and the leaders demonstrating interventions with difficult situations in a group and also a range of difficult behaviors exhibited by group members.

- You don't need to be afraid of conflict, and you don't need to have answers in advance. Be willing to remain open to group members and to encourage them to talk about their thoughts and feelings about being in the group.

- Trust the group process. If you succeed in getting members to talk about what they are thinking and feeling, the group can progress in a positive direction.

- Screening and preparing the group is essential for it lays the foundation for the future structure and development of a group. Many of the potential problems that arise as a group continues can be prevented by careful screening, preparation, and orientation before the group even convenes.

- Encourage members to speak for themselves rather than for others.

- It is essential that leaders pay attention to how members deliver their messages. Group leaders must avoid becoming defensive, even if members are exhibiting problematic behaviors.

- If there is reluctance within a group, ask what your part is contributing to members' hesitation to participate.

- Each group is different, and each group develops its own personality and moves at its own pace. Leaders do well to observe how a group evolves.

- A group is a reflection of one's own attitude as a leader. You often get what you expect. The group is influenced by the attitudes and behaviors you model as a leader.

- This program is designed to stimulate thought about ways group leaders can deal with a variety of problematic situations that occur in a group. There is no "one right way" to intervene, and leaders need to decide which approaches are most appropriate in situations they encounter.

CHECKING IN: WHAT WAS IT LIKE TO RETURN TO GROUP?

VIEW VIDEO SECTION 1: CHECKING IN: WHAT WAS IT LIKE TO RETURN TO GROUP?

Narration

The group has been meeting for several sessions. In the previous session there was conflict, and many of the members expressed a great deal of reluctance to continue attending the group. The Coreys check in with all group members to get a sense of what they are bringing to the session. This is an important step before pursuing in-depth work with any participant.

Key Points in the Group Session

Marianne checks in with members and emphasizes that she would like to hear from each member. The prior week in the group had been particularly difficult, and members were asked to think about what they are getting from the group. Marianne focuses the members by stating: "This is really a crucial moment in the group and how we will continue. I hope that each of you will make some comments, even if you say why you don't want to be here."

Your Reflections and Responses

1. What kind of focusing would you provide to give direction to a session?

_____

_____

_____

2. What would you do about a member who says during check-in "I just want to sit back and observe today?"

_____

_____

_____

Group Leaders' Reflections

The main purpose of the check-in is to hear from all members before pursuing in-depth work with any single individual. Once we have a general sense of what the members are bringing to a session, we have a direction that we can pursue. Our intention is to create an agenda with the assistance of the participants once we have heard their input. We want to teach members how they can bring themselves into the session in a meaningful way.

At this juncture we want to do what is necessary to make the room safe enough for members to talk, so we reinforce any step that members take in speaking about themselves. We take care to listen nondefensively as each member checks in.

THE LEADERS LET ME DOWN

VIEW VIDEO SECTION 2: THE LEADERS LET ME DOWN

Narration

During the check-in process, the group leaders attempt to get a sense of what members are experiencing as it pertains to being in this group and to clarify what they are willing to explore further.

Key Points in the Group Session

As the check-in begins, Galo says that he doesn't know why he has to come to the group, that he didn't feel safe in the group because he thought people were putting him down. He goes on to identify Jerry as the one he felt was putting him down.

Vivian feels the same way, claiming that she is cautious and hesitant about revealing herself. Although she wants to share a bit of herself, she does not want to reveal "too much." Marianne makes use of a scaling technique with both Galo and Vivian, asking each of them: "On a scale of 1 to 10, how ready are you to participate in this group?"

Your Reflections and Responses

1. As a leader, how would you react to Galo if he told you he was upset with you for putting him on hold?

_____

_____

_____

2. As a leader, how would you be affected if Galo told you that you had let him down?

_____

_____

_____

3. How would you respond to Vivian when she says that she is cautious and hesitant?

_____

_____

_____

4. During the check-in several members emphatically stated that they are not getting what they want, and they are not sure that they will return. As the group leader, what would you say?

_____

_____

_____

Group Leaders' Reflections

We take note of Galo saying that he was let down. However tempting it may be at that moment to continue working with Galo, at this time we want to establish who let him down, and how, and whether or not he is willing to pursue this issue later in the session. If we encourage Galo to continue exploring his reactions at this moment, this could take the entire session, and we would miss important reactions by failing to hear check-in comments from everyone.

I (Jerry) would like to know specifically how Galo feels that I let him down and what he would want from me. During the check-in process, I do not ask him to go into detail about this, but I would strongly encourage him to say more about this after everyone has had a chance to check in. I think he took an important step by saying what was on his mind. At least now I have a general sense of what may be going on with him, and I hope we can explore this issue more fully. To have a better chance of creating a safe climate, I am likely to suggest the following: "Galo, when we finish the check-in, would you be willing to say more about when you felt let down by us? I would be interested in hearing you say more about how we did not protect you, and what you would have wanted from us."

I (Marianne) wonder if Vivian is cautious because of cultural factors or lack of trust in the group. Where did she learn to be cautious in her life outside of group? How will her caution play out in this group? When Jerry asks Vivian if being cautious is something she wants change, she indicates that she would like to share a bit about herself. We want to underscore with members that the agenda for change is determined by them, not by the leaders.

Here are some possible interventions that I (Marianne) might make later on in the session:

- "Vivian, would you like to be able to talk more about yourself? Is this something you are wanting to work on in this group?"

- "Vivian, you say that you are cautious and it is hard for you to talk about yourself. When we complete the check-in, I hope that you ask for some time to say more about your hesitations and what it is like for you to be in this group. Is that something you are willing to consider doing?"

One possible intervention is to ask Vivian to talk to Galo about how she might identify with him and share a similar concern. How is watching Galo contributing to Vivian's anxiety about getting involved in the group? By asking Vivian and Galo to carry on a dialogue about their experience in the group, others may get a better picture of how each of them perceives this experience, and members might increase their awareness of how they might identify with Vivian and Galo.

I'M NOT FEELING SAFE IN HERE

VIEW VIDEO SECTION 3: I'M NOT FEELING SAFE IN HERE

Narration

Having members talk about their hesitations and difficulties pertaining to being in the group is crucial to developing trust—a sometimes tedious but necessary process.

Key Points in the Group Session

Toni says she doesn't trust anyone in the group. She has concerns about confidentiality based on a previous group experience, which makes it even more difficult for her to trust that what she says will remain within the group.

Your Reflections and Responses

1. What would you want to say to a member who states, "I don't trust people in my everyday life, and I don't trust people in this group"?

_____

_____

_____

2. What would you most want to say to the members about confidentiality and how to maintain it?

_____

_____

3. Would you raise the issue of confidentiality at the outset of group, or would you be inclined to wait until members bring it up? Explain your answer, and describe what you would say to the group about confidentiality.

_____

_____

_____

4. What would you as group leader consider a breach in group confidentiality? What will you do if confidentiality is breached?

_____

_____

_____

Group Leaders' Reflections

We need to pay close attention to Toni's feelings regarding being betrayed in a previous group as well as in life. Even if she resolves this issue with the group at this time, we wonder when her concerns about maintaining trust will reappear. We also wonder who in her life has disappointed her and if this might lead to some future work for her in this group. A question we may pose to Toni is how she dealt with the previous group when confidentiality was broken. We want to be sure to challenge her to express any concerns she might have about confidentiality at any point in this group.

Jerry's rationale for asking Toni about her level of trust outside the group gives a sense of how pervasive the issue of trust is for Toni and the importance of exploring this issue within the group. Note that Toni is asked if her lack of trusting and lack of feeling safe is something that she would like to change. If Toni is not interested in learning to trust more fully, then it might be futile to try to convince her that she should be more trusting. However, when she says that she would like to change this in her life, we have a direction to pursue. It is up to the member to decide what he or she wants from being in the group.

Toni's concern about trust seems to be related to both her experience in this group and also in her everyday life. When someone states a here-and-now concern pertaining to the group, we often want to get a better understanding of how the theme may be operating in their day-to-day living. It gives us an idea of what they might want to focus on within the group and what ways they might want to change, both in and outside of group.

As leaders, we cannot guarantee that confidentiality will always be honored by members of the group. We can only reassure members that we will work hard to emphasize the importance of maintaining a sense of confidentiality.

I DIDN'T WANT TO COME BACK TO GROUP
VIEW VIDEO SECTION 4: I DIDN'T WANT TO COME BACK TO GROUP

Narration
The unwillingness to participate can be expected at an early stage, especially with involuntary group members.

Key Points in the Group Session
Joel states: "Well, I was reluctant to come back this week because I felt that last week I shared a lot, and I was feeling guilty about this."

Like Joel, Nicole says that she is reluctant to talk. Nicole expresses that it is difficult to open up when others don't want to be present in the group.

Maria did not want to come back because she feels so different from others. Maria is nervous about speaking out as a member of the group when other group members are so articulate. She is afraid others will judge her for the way she speaks, so she does not want to say anything.

Your Reflections and Responses
1. How would you work with a member who is reluctant to return?

_____

_____

_____

2. How would you address Joel's guilt about having taken up too much time and having disclosed too much?

_____

_____

_____

3. Nicole says that she is going to be quiet and observe others until she starts hearing from some of the other members. How would you address that?

_____

_____

_____

4. How would you address Maria's fear about the way she speaks?

_____

_____

_____

Group Leaders' Reflections
When members share concerns about their reasons for not wanting to return to the group, we strive to listen nondefensively to their concerns and not to discount what they are saying. If members are blaming us for their dissatisfaction with the group and do not want to come back, it is crucial that we listen respectfully to what they are saying. It is important to recognize that they did come back to the group and that they are talking about this matter. We want to acknowledge that they have taken a positive step.

Joel has a trust issue in that he was afraid to return to the group. He felt concerned that he shared too much in the previous session, and now he is wondering how people might perceive him and react to him. Oftentimes members are reluctant to return or to participate after they have shared a good deal about themselves in a particular session. This may be due to a number of factors such as embarrassment, uncertainty about confidentiality, betraying those spoken about, or anxiety about what people are thinking. We will not know what a member's reasons are for feeling reluctant to return unless we ask about this and provide the person with an opportunity to express these concerns to us and to the members in the group.

I'M IN THIS GROUP AGAINST MY WILL
VIEW VIDEO SECTION 5: I'M IN THIS GROUP AGAINST MY WILL

Narration
As the group progresses, trust continues to be a major issue. Genuine feedback and encouragement from members and leaders can help involuntary members to become more involved.

Key Points in the Group Session
Nadine talks about her fear in that she is training to be a professional counselor, and yet now she is in the role of a client. She states that she is afraid that people who see her as a professional will laugh at her because she is also a client.

Galo expresses his reactions to George. Galo is hesitant to talk about his private life if George continues in his stance of expressing lack of interest.

Nicole tells both Nadine and George that she would have more respect for them if they were to share more and that she has a hard time with them shutting down.

Joel makes it known that he wants to be accepted by the males in the group, and he feels judged by George.

Marianne asks George how it is for him to hear what Joel is saying. George examines what he can learn from this experience. He is beginning to see a connection to how he is at home and in this group. George is asking himself about how much he listens and cares.

Jerry is encouraging George to look at his behavior in the here-and-now of this group that might teach him more about how he is at home.

George says that he is learning something about himself. He realizes that there is no way he will be able to get through this experience without getting involved if his words are going to have an effect on others. George gets more emotional and says he wants to continue in the group. He becomes more open to the idea that he can get something useful for himself from the group. He indicates that maybe at home he won't have to go lock himself in his office, but instead he can hear what others are telling him.

Joel responds to George—"You showed me a different side of yourself, and now I can trust you more. I am less afraid of being judged by you and Galo now that I have heard more from you both. Now I feel I can share more of myself in here and not feel guilty or worry about being judged."

Marianne asks George: "So, if you had to decide at this time whether to continue with this group or deal with the consequences, where do you think you'd be?" George reflects on this question and replies: "I'd like to continue coming because of the shift in what is happening to me right now."

Nadine feels the group is not up to her level of sophistication, and she was required to attend by her graduate program. Her program chair thinks she needs personal therapy, but Nadine does not see the value of personal self-disclosure. She would rather assume an observational stance and learn about group process and about client dynamics. She does not see the relevance of working on her own personal issues. In many respects, Nadine is an involuntary member.

Like Nadine, George is not coming to the group because this is something he wants for himself. George is attending group because of his wife's ultimatum. Marianne asks what will happen if he doesn't attend, and George then explores the consequences of nonattendance.

Jerry and Marianne talk to Nadine and George about their reluctance to participate in the group. Marianne goes on to tell both Nadine and George that she is concerned for them if they continue coming to this group but see no value in being a part of the experience. She says, "I would hope you take care of yourself and not continue coming if you do not want to be here."

Your Reflections and Responses

1. If Nadine told you in a pregroup screening session that she was attending only because she was required to by her faculty, would you have accepted her into the group? Explain why or why not?

_____

_____

_____

2. Can you think of ways to work with Nadine so that she could benefit from the group, even though her attendance is mandatory?

_____

_____

_____

3. Marianne says to George with some humor, "Well, you really did come here because doing so would be better than facing the ultimatum with your wife. Nobody dragged you in here." Do you see any value in humor? How do you determine when humor is appropriate or inappropriate?

_____

_____

_____

4. Based on your observations of how Marianne worked with George, how might you have worked with him differently?

_____

_____

_____

Group Leaders' Reflections

In groups that we lead, it is our practice to conduct individual screening interviews for selection and orientation purposes. We also hold a pregroup session with all the potential members. This is done for the purpose of making sure that the members' goals match our goals for the group. We want to make sure that members are well informed about what they can expect from the group.

Many times group leaders may be confronted with being assigned a mandatory group. In these cases, it may not be possible to screen the members, nor even to prepare them for a group experience. In this situation the challenge is to create an environment in which involuntary members can recognize that there could be potential personal benefits from participating in a group.

Both Nadine and George are examples of involuntary members who, as a result of expressing their hesitations and doubts about being asked to attend the group, eventually were able to recognize that there could be some personal value for them by participating in the group. It is crucial to avoid becoming defensive and combative with such members, and to intervene appropriately with other members' reactions to the involuntary members.

Involuntary members need to know that they are free to leave the group. However, leaders would do well to find out from the reluctant members what the consequences will be for them if they choose not to attend, and then to challenge them with their choices in a nonjudgmental way. It is the involuntary group member who needs to deal with the consequences of not participating, not the leaders or the other group members. For example, I (Marianne) do not argue with George or try to convince him that he needs therapy. Instead, I ask him to talk about what it was like for him to be in the group that he did not seek out voluntarily. My focus is on bringing to his awareness that even though he was coerced by his wife to attend the group, he did indeed choose to come.

It is important that Nadine and George explore what they are thinking and feeling about being asked by someone else to come the group. If they are willing to talk about what it is like to be sent to the group, then there is a chance they might want to revise this and look for some ways they can get involved in the group for themselves. They do have a choice of whether or not they will continue in this group, and it is important that they do not stay in the group if they really see no value for themselves. We have concerns about having members remain in a group if they are not willing to invest themselves in a personal way. Participation could be more harmful than helpful to both George and Nadine if they feel forced and do not recognize that they had some degree of choice in this matter. If either of them continue their stance of feeling coerced to remain in the group, we are likely to provide them with a referral to alternative resources. For George, it could be marriage counseling. For Nadine, it might be seeking other ways of learning about group process or to deal with the faculty who required her to join the group.

Nicole has reactions to Nadine (and also to George) who are saying they don't want to share themselves personally. I (Jerry) am particularly interested in why Nadine's and George's level of participation is a concern for Nicole. I would challenge Nicole to say more about herself and why it is important for her to hear more from members who are reluctant to self-disclose. In some ways Nicole gives only part of her message. She needs to let members know why hearing from them is important to her.

George is making a connection between his behavior at home and in this group. I (Marianne) am thinking that George could make productive use of the group by exploring how he is in here as a way to show him more about how he functions at home. If George recognizes that he does not listen or care the way he wants to, then he can use the group as a place to work on changing this pattern in himself. There is a shift in George when he realizes that he will not be able to get through the group without getting personally involved. I want to be sure to bring to his awareness what happened when he talked and did not run away or shut people out. I would encourage him to say more about how he might see himself getting more involved. At this point George has been with the members for several sessions, and he has some sense about them. An intervention I might make is to ask, "George, would you tell different people here in what ways you'd like to be more involved with them?"

This is a critical turning point for George and illustrates how members can make a shift in attitude from being an unwilling to a willing participant. It is important to reinforce George's openness that leads to a different decision on his part. I (Marianne) want George to recognize that by letting us know that he did not want to be a part of the group, it was possible for him to get to the place where he is now. I tell the group that by taking the step to talk about what makes it difficult to be in the group, they have a better chance to get to a different place than if they do not say anything at all.

George admits that he is somewhat scared and that something powerful happened to him. One way George might continue is by talking more about his fears about getting more personal. I (Marianne) may suggest a go-around where George completes this sentence: "I am afraid to become personal with you because. . . ." This experiment can provide George, as well as all of us, with a greater awareness of his fears and how his anxiety can get in his way. His tendency to shut people out is most likely to happen at different junctures, especially when he is uncomfortable in a session. He did see some results when he was different with people and did not shut them out. If he were to shut people out again, I am likely to remind him of what happened when he allowed himself to open up to people and talk about his fears. Although it was difficult for him to do this, he did value the outcomes.

George also says that he is learning that perhaps there is another way for him to be at home rather than lock himself in his office and shut down. At some point I (Jerry) may intervene by inviting George to symbolically bring his wife into this group by suggesting: "George, would you pick someone in here who could represent your wife and tell her now what goes on with you when you keep yourself locked in your room? Perhaps you can say more to her about how you would like to be different." Of course, my interventions are always created by listening to what George is saying and looking for opportunities to encourage him to bring his outside concerns into this group. I am likely to suggest this experiment with George especially if he indicates that he is not satisfied with how he interacts with his wife and that he would like to be different.

With Joel, I (Jerry) am listening to ways of linking his work with both George and Galo. Joel is providing an opening with his feedback to George when he says to him that he is less afraid of being judged as weak if he shares about himself. As a possible intervention, I may ask Joel to say more to both George and Galo about himself, especially aspects regarding being weak and being judged, which he might want to explore in future sessions. At some point I would encourage him to address how these issues are problematic for him outside of the group.

EMOTIONS MAKE ME UNCOMFORTABLE

VIEW VIDEO SECTION 6: EMOTIONS MAKE ME UNCOMFORTABLE

Narration

Sometimes a group member is uncomfortable with other members' emotions. Toni completes a go-around telling the members what she wants from them, and group members continue to share their difficulty in communicating with each other.

Key Points in the Group Session

Vivian is put off by the emotions of group members and would like for them to feel better quickly. She is uncomfortable with the emotions of others (especially crying) and with her own emotions. Her tendency is to stop the tears of others.

Toni lets Vivian know that she was triggered by Vivian's comment on not trusting others with her tears. Toni admits that she has a big wall around her and that it is difficult for her to make herself emotionally vulnerable. Toni talks about letting down the wall—one brick at a time. She adds that even though she would like to take down some of her wall, she is not sure how to do that.

Marianne acknowledges to Toni that she is taking down some bricks by talking and relating to others in here. Marianne suggests to Toni that she tell each of us what she wants or needs that would make it safer for her to talk and also to let down some of the wall.

Your Reflections and Responses

1. What possible cultural messages are relevant to explore with Vivian regarding her hesitation to express emotions?

_____

_____

_____

2. How would you assist Vivian in dealing with her reactions to emotions displayed by others?

_____

_____

3. Could Vivian benefit from the group even though she operated more on a cognitive level than an emotional level? Explain your answer.

_____

_____

4. When Vivian says that she is not accustomed to seeing people cry and wants to make them feel better, how would you work with that? If Vivian tells you that she does not want to change this behavior, how would you respond?

_____

_____

_____

5. What did the Coreys do to facilitate Toni in establishing more trust and safety? What would you say to her?

_____

_____

_____

Group Leaders' Reflections

Members who are uncomfortable with the emotions of others are also generally anxious about experiencing their own emotions. As leaders, it is not our task to insist that members should experience and express their emotions. We need to be cognizant of a potential bias that genuine work occurs only with emotional intensity. Many members are able to benefit from a group even though they may never express themselves emotionally. Instead, their work is primarily cognitive. We need to intervene, however, if members are trying to sabotage the emotional work of other members. We take our cues from members if they want to integrate cognitive and emotional work.

In the case of Vivian, we are likely to ask her to talk more about what she is experiencing with particular members as they are expressing emotions. We might facilitate this work by suggesting that Vivian talk directly to the members who are contributing to Vivian's anxiety by telling the members more about herself. Our agenda is not to get Vivian to become more emotional, unless she indicates that she would like to be able to identify and experience more of her own emotions. Yet we do think it is important that Vivian puts into words some of her reactions as other members work. If Vivian does not talk about this, there is a chance that she could become overwhelmed by her own anxiety, which is triggered by others' emotional work. This could affect Vivian negatively.

Like Vivian, Toni is also affected by the emotional work of others. Toni has fears about experiencing emotions and erects walls to protect herself from being hurt. Toni states that she would like to be able to operate on a more emotional level when it is appropriate. We first ask Toni to talk about what she experiences (her own thoughts and feelings) as she listens to others. We initiate a go-around in which Toni can say something specific to each member, especially what it is like for her to have protective walls. What would Toni want from each person? What would help her to feel increased safety? By participating in the go-around, Toni is taking another step in the direction of making herself known to us. This is indicated when she says that she wants to let down her wall somewhat. Before we would focus on bringing her wall down, we would begin with what she would need from each of us to feel safer in group.

Future work with Toni could include having her reflect on what made her build these protective walls, what she imagines might happen if she lowers her shield, and to whom in her life she might want to make herself more vulnerable. We would check with Toni before pursuing this line of work because earlier she indicated that she is having trouble feeling trust and safety in the group. We want to provide a context in which Toni will be able to experiment with letting her wall down. Again, this is not our agenda; Toni is indicating that she would like to be more open and more emotionally expressive.

I'M SELF-CONSCIOUS ABOUT MY ACCENT

VIEW VIDEO SECTION 7: I'M SELF-CONSCIOUS ABOUT MY ACCENT

Narration

The group leaders ask members to express their reactions. Galo has reactions to what he perceives as Nicole's attitude. Although he tells her he does not like her tone with others (her "attitude"), he wants to dismiss her and does not want to continue talking to her. Marianne facilitates Galo talking directly to Nicole, and then asks Nicole to respond to how it is for her to hear what Galo tells her.

Key Points in the Group Session

Maria expresses (to Nicole) how uncomfortable she feels in talking because she wonders if others have difficulty understanding her due to her accent.

Nicole responds defensively with, "See this is why I don't want to talk in here because now it is my fault that Maria doesn't participate." Nicole quickly responds that if Maria is concerned about being understood because of her accent, then it is Maria's problem and Nicole doesn't want it put on her. Marianne challenges Nicole not to withdraw, but to continue talking to Maria and keeping the dialogue open.

Your Reflections and Responses

1. What would you want to say to Maria regarding her fear of not being understood because of her accent?

_____

_____

_____

2. You ask Nicole not to withdraw, yet she crosses her arms and curtly says, "I'm not going to say anything more." How would you deal with this stance?

_____

_____

_____

3. What do you imagine would happen if Marianne challenged Galo and Nicole to continue to talk? How might that affect Galo and Nicole? The other members? You?

_____

_____

_____

Group Leaders' Reflections

Although the focus of this part of the session began with Maria saying that she was concerned about the degree to which others are able to understand her because of her accent, the focus shifted to Nicole and to Galo. This occurred because Nicole reacted defensively to Maria, and then Galo had reactions to Nicole's "attitude." If we do not attend to these reactions, there will be a lack of trust that is not conducive to Maria's exploration of how her accent affects her participation in this group and how her accent also influences her in daily life. It is important to address Nicole and Galo's reactions and to attend to what is going on, but it is equally important that we come back to Maria so that she has time to talk more about her concerns over her accent, and also how she might be reacting to Nicole and Galo's interchange.

As coleaders we are hoping that Galo is not going to shut Nicole out and keep his anger about her "attitude" to himself. We facilitate a way to guide him in saying more about how he is affected by Nicole. I (Marianne) want Galo to express directly to Nicole how he perceives her and where that leaves him. Eventually Galo says to Nicole that he is put off by her flippant attitude. With prompting, Galo tells Nicole that what he wants from her is that she "tries to curb down her attitude and listen." Once Galo has expressed himself to Nicole, it is important that Nicole has an opportunity to say what she heard Galo say and how it was for her to hear his message. We encourage members to let others know how they are being affected by each other, rather than judging one another.

I (Marianne) observe that several members have reactions to the way Nicole responds to them. They seem put off by her giving bottom-line messages, but often leaving out parts of her message that might be easier to listen to and evoke less defensiveness in others. While members are confronting Nicole about her "attitude," as a leader I may want to call to her attention how often she evokes defensiveness in others by the way she interacts with them. I encourage Nicole to pay attention to how others in this group are reacting to her and to reflect on whether her interpersonal style is working for her. Some of her future work might entail exploring how effective her interpersonal style is away from the group.

VIEW VIDEO SECTION 8: I WANT THE LEADERS TO DISCLOSE MORE

Narration

Sometimes in a group setting there is a pressure for leaders to self-disclose. In this section the group leaders continue reacting to the members' pressures for the leaders to self-disclose.

Key Points in the Group Session

Nicole observes that we are all expected to share and be personal, but she doesn't hear anything personal from the coleaders. She wonders what makes the leaders so different and asks the group leaders to share more about themselves. Jerry and Marianne respond to her request by stating their views on leader self-disclosure.

In essence, Jerry agrees that he won't be sharing a great deal of his personal life because he has a different job in the group. However, he does want to share his reactions to what is happening in the sessions and his reactions to different members. Marianne responds with: "I want to be very personal, but you probably won't learn a lot about my personal problems. I want to share my reactions, and I hope you will learn about me as the group goes on."

Your Reflections and Responses

1. As a group leader, how would you have handled Nicole's challenge to you of being nondisclosing?

_____

_____

_____

2. How would you deal with direct questions about your life?

_____

_____

_____

3. What difference do you see in disclosing your personal history versus sharing your here-and-now reactions in the context of the group?

_____

_____

_____

Group Leaders' Reflections

As coleaders we are often asked by members to become more personally involved in the group by sharing more of our personal lives with them. Sometimes members are simply curious about us, and we are likely to answer some of their questions. At other times, their probing for us to self-disclose could involve their attempt to feel comfortable with us and establish trust with us. We are very willing to disclose our ongoing reactions and observations about them as well as how we are affected by them. Generally, we do not explore or try to solve our personal problems in the groups we are leading. We find it difficult to be present for members if we consistently indulge in talking about our out-of-group concerns. We do not display an attitude that we are problem-free because we are leaders and that *they* are the ones with the problems. At times we may identify with certain clients who evoke personal reactions in us, and we tend to acknowledge the effect they are having on us. However, we are not likely to work in greater depth on our personal issues. We hope the members can perceive us as vulnerable human beings without our having to prove that we are human by being overly self-disclosing.

VIEW VIDEO SECTION 9: I LEARN A LOT BY BEING QUIET

Narration

Quiet members can affect the trust level in a group, and leaders need to explore the meaning for their silence. The focus shifts to a group member who still feels left out.

Key Points in the Group Session

Vivian observes that she is a quiet member, and she adds that she would like to learn how to be a bit more verbally expressive. She adds that she did not like Jerry's comment earlier that there are consequences to her being quiet in the group.

Galo feels left out because he didn't get an opportunity to talk. However, he adds that he does not want the focus on him, and that he finds it anxiety provoking to ask for time in a session. He would prefer not initiating, but having the leaders call on him. Galo adds that if he were to take time for himself he would feel that he is depriving others of their time. He admits that in his daily life he tends to focus on meeting the needs of others, and he typically does not ask for time for himself. Although it makes him anxious to speak up, he is willing to consider the idea to do so.

Your Reflections and Responses

1. Jerry tells Vivian that there are consequences to keeping her thoughts, feelings, and reactions to herself. If she says little about herself and does not share her reactions, other members are likely to have reactions to her. Jerry also intervenes by telling Vivian that it will pose difficulties if she does all of her work quietly. What are your thoughts about Jerry's comments to Vivian?

_____

_____

_____

2. If Vivian were to tell you that she learns best by observing the process quietly, how would you respond?

_____

_____

_____

3. Marianne intervenes with Vivian by telling her, "I hope you won't let anyone pressure you into doing anything that does not feel right for you. You need to be clear about what your goals are for yourself in this group. Others may have reactions to you if you are quiet, but the most important thing is that you take care of yourself so you won't have regrets." What are your thoughts regarding Marianne's intervention?

_____

_____

_____

4. After hearing Galo identify his anxiety about talking in the group, would you be willing to call on him? Why or why not?

_____

_____

_____

5. How would you intervene if other members interpreted Galo's quietness as meaning that he is judging them? What specifically will you say?

_____

_____

_____

Group Leaders' Reflections

Vivian has reactions to Jerry when he says that there are consequences for not talking about herself in the group. I (Jerry) appreciate that Vivian lets me know that she is put off by my remark about consequences for members who are quiet. This allows me to clarify what I meant by "consequences." Vivian understood my reference to consequences differently from what I intended to communicate. I am able to clarify to her that if she keeps most of her reactions to herself, others are likely left guessing about how she is being affected by them. Often members will project onto a quiet member.

I (Marianne) agree with Jerry challenging Vivian to verbally participate; however, I also want to emphasize to her that she has a choice in this matter. At the same time, I want to encourage her to take the necessary steps and risks to accomplish the goals she has set out for herself. Some possible future work might well be her strong reactions to the term "consequences." I would not want to discount her reactions to Jerry and his choice of words, yet I also wonder if there might be some historical vestiges that warrant further exploration.

I (Jerry) suggest to Galo that he explore the issues of taking time for himself in the group sessions. I explain to Galo that I am hesitant to call on him because this will deprive him of the opportunity to decide when to participate and what to reveal. By waiting to be called upon, Galo does not always get what he wants unless other people initiate the communication. I encourage Galo to take the first step by admitting that he is scared and is uncomfortable with being the focus of attention, but nevertheless he will commit himself to asking for time. This would be a useful place for Galo to begin challenging his fears. However, there might be powerful cultural messages about taking the lead and bringing himself into a group session, and this, too, is something that he could explore. As leaders, we do not see it as our place to challenge cultural injunctions, but we provide members with an opportunity to determine for themselves whether they want to experiment with changing a cultural message. Galo admits that he gets very anxious just thinking about asking for time in the group. As I listen to Galo, I am thinking of how much he can actually give to others by taking time to talk about matters that are of significance to him. His work could easily be a catalyst for others. If Galo agrees that initiating and asking for time in a group is something he is willing to do, ideas for future work could entail encouraging him to speak up first in subsequent sessions, providing him with opportunities to practice asking others to listen to him, and exploring some of the messages he hears that keep him from making his presence be known.

COMMENTARY

VIEW VIDEO SECTION COMMENTARY

Key Points in the Commentary

- Do everything you can to get members to talk about trust in the group.
- Ask members to identify what it is like for them to be in this group.
- It is essential that members talk about what makes it difficult for them to participate in the sessions. Their willingness to talk about their reluctance is a positive step in the direction of moving forward as a group.
- Coming back to group the next week is a big step for the members to make. It is important for leaders to acknowledge the members for showing up, in spite of the fact that some of them weren't sure if they wanted to continue. Now the members need to be willing to say aloud what makes it difficult for them to be a part of this group.

- Demonstrate respectful challenge and recognize that it is a positive step in creating trust when members verbalize their difficulties.

- Safety is a critical issue, and it can be assessed by noting the willingness of members to take risks by expressing their thoughts and reactions. The main intervention is to motivate members to talk, especially about what gives them difficulty in the group context.

- There are no techniques to get members to talk more, other than group leaders making it safe for members to say difficult things. How the leaders respond to what members say and the risks they take is a major factor in establishing trust.

- There is no one right way to intervene, and leaders are encouraged to reflect on what they expect to get from the interventions they make. It may help to let the members know the rationale for some of the things leaders are expecting from the members.

- As a leader, avoid becoming defensive in listening to group members' grievances.

- It is useful to teach members to bring themselves into the group interaction when they are affected by someone, rather than waiting to be called upon. The leader will not know how and when members are affected by others unless they do take this step to let others know about their experience in the here and now.

- Appreciate the difficulty that many group members have; don't label it resistance. Find ways to reframe resistance and to use descriptive language rather than judgmental language. It is helpful to assist members in identifying ways they may be reluctant and to explore their defenses.

- It is not the leader's job to decide how members should change. Instead, the members need to figure out what kinds of behaviors they want to modify. Leaders need to consistently work with members to get them to state what they want to talk about in the group sessions and what they want for themselves. Cultural differences need to be considered in expecting members to change certain behaviors.

- It is important to encourage members to talk about what is difficult for them to say. If they are scared, can they acknowledge this? If they find it difficult to ask for time, can they state this? If they fear judgment from others, can they talk about this concern? When members say they are closed off or are not trusting, ask if they would like to change this. Members bring themselves into the here and now by talking about what they are aware of presently, and then taking some critical steps to move forward.

IN-CLASS EXERCISE: QUESTIONS FOR SMALL GROUP DISCUSSION AND REFLECTING TEAMS

Form reflecting teams in small groups within your class. This can be done as an entire class activity if the group is small enough. Now that you have viewed the first nine scenarios of this program, each illustrating a particular theme, share your observations and reactions. It is important for you to avoid judging, diagnosing, and interpreting. For instance, avoid labeling a member as being "passive aggressive," or trying to figure out hidden motivations for what an individual says or does.

In your small group, focus on what you heard and saw, on what stood out for you, and the most salient moments of the program thus far. The aim of the reflecting team is to share your thoughts, feelings, and reactions to what you are seeing unfold in the group and to reflect on your experience of observing the various vignettes. Pay particular attention to how you are personally affected by the members and the leaders, and how that might influence the way you would lead this group. Doing this can bring to your awareness your potential countertransference issues, which you may or may not share with your reflecting team.

1. What steps could you take to increase the feeling of safety in a group, especially when members say they don't feel safe?

2. Which group member(s) would you find most challenging to work with in this group? Explain.

3. What thoughts do you have about members who are mandated to attend your groups?

4. How would you work with members who claim they are very uncomfortable expressing and exploring emotion?

5. What cultural issues most caught your attention in these sections of the video?

VIEW VIDEO SECTION 10: SILENCE SERVES A FUNCTION

Narration

As the session continues, the Coreys encourage the participants to explore their difficulties with one another.

Key Points in the Group Session

Jerry makes an intervention by raising a question: "So, who else is ready to do more?" Members are silent, and Marianne wonders what the hesitation is about. She asks members to reflect on what makes it difficult for them to talk and to say something about what it is like for them to be in this group right now. Some time elapses before the first person speaks.

Your Reflections and Responses

1. Would you have been inclined to allow the silence to go on until someone finally spoke up? Explain.

_____

_____

_____

2. What reactions might you have if there were long silences in a group you were leading?

_____

_____

_____

Group Leaders' Reflections

As we notice the hesitation to speak, we are interested in pursuing what it is that members are not saying but perhaps thinking. Silence in a group is not necessarily problematic, and it may serve a useful purpose. Members need a pause to get centered and to reflect. Moments of silence can afford the space for members to get focused and to reflect on what they are experiencing. However, there are also nonproductive silences, which may be characterized by withholding thoughts, feelings, and reactions. It is important for leaders to assess the meaning of members' silence.

The silence could have many possible meanings; here are a few reasons a group may become silent:

- Members do not know how to initiate in a group or how to interact in a group.
- Members are frightened or are having difficulty in trusting.
- Members are reluctant to have the focus of attention.
- Members are intimidated by other members or by the group leaders.
- Members are responding to cultural messages not to be noticed and not to stand out.
- Members are responding to the pressure to verbally participate.
- Members may lack confidence that they have anything worthwhile to say.

I FEEL PRESSURED TO DISCLOSE

VIEW VIDEO SECTION 11: I FEEL PRESSURED TO DISCLOSE

Narration

After a silence in the group session, Joel is the first to speak. He thinks the leaders are asking too many questions and that he is being pressured to talk and reveal personal material. He is critical of all the questions that are coming from the group leaders. He says that he wants to go at his own pace.

Key Points in the Group Session

Marianne encourages Joel to express his dislike of the leaders' questions and asks him to verbalize this whenever he feels the leaders are not helping. The leaders do not react to Joel's expression of emotion, but rather facilitate discussion of his concerns.

Your Reflections and Responses

1. At the beginning of this session, there was a silence. If the silence continued for some time after you made an opening statement, what might you be inclined to say or do? If members do not respond to the invitation to participate, what would be the next step for you?

_____

_____

2. How might you respond to Joel's challenge to you as a leader that you are pressuring him? How will you respond to Joel when he says, in essence, "leave me alone"?

_____

_____

_____

3. Is it possible to conduct a therapeutic group without pressure of any kind? How would you distinguish between ethical and unethical group pressure? What kinds of interventions can you think of to help hesitant members accomplish their goals?

_____

_____

_____

4. How can you communicate to members that they have choices about participation and, at the same time, challenge them to take the risks necessary to bring about change?

_____

_____

_____

5. How can you determine whether members are helped or hindered by their group attendance if they are hesitant to express themselves? What ethical issues are involved here?

_____

_____

_____

Group Leaders' Reflections

As leaders, we want to invite Joel to say more about the pressure he experiences from the group leaders. He states that he wants to be left alone and go at his own pace. Although we can certainly respect Joel's wish to go at his own pace, we do have concerns about his request to leave him alone. We would give him our reasons for our concerns if he wanted to remain in the group. At this juncture, we may want to renegotiate his original goals that he hoped to accomplish through group participation. We do have an expectation that Joel will talk about what it is like for him to be in this group. This includes expressing what might impede his trust and willingness to participate.

With respect to future work, it may be productive to ask Joel to explore his feelings about being pressured, both in this group and in daily life. Who, if anyone, might be impatient with him in his life?

WHAT'S WRONG WITH HELPING OTHERS?

VIEW VIDEO SECTION 12: WHAT'S WRONG WITH HELPING OTHERS?

Narration

Another challenge to group leaders occurs when a member takes on the role of a coleader.

Key Points in the Group Session

Nadine intervenes by commenting on Joel's behavior, and also defends the leaders' interventions. She tends to make observations and interpretations about others rather than talk about herself. Nicole responds to Nadine by saying, "It makes me think that you are not here to work on yourself, but you just want to be one of the leaders." Marianne asks Nadine to reflect on her style of intervening to determine if this is why she is in the group.

Your Reflections and Responses

1. How would you react to Nicole's confrontation with Nadine? What would you say to facilitate their interaction?

2. If a member of your group (such as Nadine) were assuming the role of a coleader, what direction would you pursue?

Group Leaders' Reflections

Members sometimes develop an interpersonal style of taking on the role of assistant leaders. They may demonstrate a variety of behaviors such as frequently asking questions, probing for information, giving advice to other members, and trying to "fix others." Such members tend to pay attention to the dynamics of the group, and they focus more on others in the group than on themselves. Instead of paying attention to how they may be affected in the group, they shift the focus to others by making interventions and assuming a counselor's role. This behavior tends to evoke a strong reaction from other participants. It is necessary to deal with this problematic behavior because it is likely to be resented by the other members, and it often impedes the progress of a group. Furthermore, members who takes refuge in adopting such a role are deprived of the opportunity to work on the concerns that brought them to the group in the first place.

Recognizing this behavior as a possible defense, the leader can sensitively block it by pointing out to such members that they are depriving themselves of the maximum benefit from the group by paying more attention to others than to themselves. They joined the group to explore their own concerns, and they can lose sight of this goal if they leave themselves out of the process by constantly taking on the role of a group leader. Although their intention is often to be helpful to others, it tends to deprive them of working on their own personal goals. It is essential that these members not be chastised or dismissed for their way of interacting, but instead be asked to look at the possible motivations for their behavior.

As was the case with Nadine, a member's intention to be helpful can have a negative effect. In working with Nadine, we ponder the following questions for understanding her behavior: Could her helpfulness be a defense to keep her from dealing with her own problems? Is being helpful a major part of her personality outside of the group, and if so, does she see any reason to change this? Is being helpful getting her what she wants in her life? Might her behavior imply that she does not trust that the leaders are doing an adequate job? Might she be rescuing the group leaders because they are being confronted by other members? Might her style of assisting us as coleaders be a way of sabotaging the group's movement into a direction that is too threatening to her? How can we help Nadine in dealing with the reactions other members are having toward her? All these questions we file away and pursue with Nadine at a later point in the group. We don't want to overwhelm Nadine with too much feedback, but we do hope she will take a look at how much she is getting for herself by assuming more of an observer's role than that of a participant.

VIEW VIDEO SECTION 13: CAN'T WE STOP ALL THIS CONFLICT?

Narration

A lot of energy is being stirred up with just about all of the members in the group. When conflicts exist, leaders must carefully monitor the members' interactions.

Leaders need to challenge members to keep the focus on how they are being affected, rather than blaming others for what they are feeling. The leaders use the group process as a way to understand and explore the conflict. As a result of not bypassing conflict and continuing to talk, members begin to have a better understanding of each other.

Key Points in the Group Session

A number of members begin expressing how they are feeling about the tension in the room. Toni and Nadine are arguing about who is correct. Nicole focuses on what Nadine is doing and blaming her for Nicole's unwillingness to be more open. Joel sees the group as splitting and wants the leaders to do something about the tension. George wants to be left out of the interchanges, stating that he doesn't like all this tension flying around and does not even want to be in here right now. Vivian is giving explanations for the conflict. The leaders allow the conflict to emerge and do not immediately intervene.

Toni says Nicole was attacked by Nadine. Toni raises her voice and asks, "Don't you feel attacked?"

After several heated interchanges, Marianne asks the members to consider what is going on now and what is being evoked in each one of them. She notes that it is important to look at what the irritation and impatience with one another means. Although some of the members want to move on, Marianne urges members to keep talking and not avoid dealing with the conflict. Marianne also says that it is important to look at what is bringing about the intense energy in the room.

Vivian says she wants to get away from the conflict. Vivian expresses that she does not like conflict, that she comes to a person's rescue, and that she tries not to have conflict at all. If there is conflict, she wants it resolved as quickly as possible. Marianne reminds Vivian of an earlier statement she made about how to stay with conflict and see it through is something she wanted to learn and apply in her everyday life.

Marianne instructs members about the importance of sticking with a conflict and continuing to talk about themselves and looks for reactions from members.

Nicole seems to have an insight about the intensity of her reactions to Nadine. Nicole expresses a parent issue with Nadine. Nicole admits that she has issues with her parents when they asked a lot of questions and gave a lot of advice, yet never gave a lot of themselves personally. Marianne intervenes with Nicole by asking Nicole to let Nadine know what it is like for her when she hears her questions and advice.

Marianne challenges Nicole to notice the changes Nadine is making in the way she is talking at this moment, rather than continuing to chastise Nadine.

Marianne gives Nadine the feedback that although she wants to be helpful, several people are telling her that she is not helping them.

Jerry reminds Nadine that earlier she said that she wanted to fix things with people and that this wears her out. He asks her if she is successful in her attempts and if this behavior is working for her. The coleaders ask Nadine if she wants to change this style of behaving.

Nadine addresses her pain with others when she says, "It is painful for me not to be able to fix people's problems."

Marianne intervenes with Nadine by asking her to complete the sentence, "It is painful for me not to be able to fix. . . ." She then addresses each person in the group.

Vivian enters in by saying that she tends to think first and then have feelings later. Jerry suggests to Vivian that rather than think about things first, it may be helpful for her to express her immediate feelings that come up for her in the group.

Marianne says to Vivian, "Watch out! Watch out for him. He is proposing something to you. Is this what you want?" Marianne emphasizes to Vivian: "I'm proposing to you that you pay attention to what is it in you that you want to change."

Vivian reveals that she tries to connect with people, but she does so more on a cognitive level than a feeling level. She lets Maria know that she is trying to connect with her, but what works for her best is to engage her in an intellectual way. Vivian follows the leaders' suggestion to make the rounds and say something to each member about how she tries to connect with each person on a thinking level.

Your Reflections and Responses

1. What would you want to say to Toni when she interjects with, "Don't you feel attacked?" What is your hunch about Toni's thinking when she asks that question?

_____

_____

_____

2. What might you say to George when he says, "I don't want to be in this room right now. This bickering is making me tense, and I want to leave?"

_____

_____

_____

3. Vivian says she wants to get away from the conflict and she wants to leave. What would say to her?

_____

_____

_____

4. Joel requests that the group leaders to do something about this conflict. If you were the group leader, what kind of intervention would you make?

_____

_____

_____

Group Leaders' Reflections

Toni says, with a great deal of energy, that Nadine was attacking Nicole by assuming a superior attitude. We focus Toni more on herself and what her strong reactions reveal about her. We might intervene with a statement to Toni somewhat like this: "You are obviously affected by what you perceive as an attack by Nadine. What do you suppose your intense reaction might be saying about you?" In short, we are trying to teach members the importance of talking about their own reactions and staying away from telling others how they are.

It is interesting for us to note that Nadine does evoke some reactions in other members. Joel sees her as questioning other members, Nicole views her as wanting to be an extra leader, and Toni sees Nadine as attacking Nicole. We are not yet sure what all this means. However, a direction we want to pursue is having each member speak for him- or herself. I (Marianne) hope that Nicole will look more at herself, especially some possible transference reaction she may be having toward Nadine.

We want members to talk about how they are being affected by each other rather than blaming others or judging others' behavior. For instance, we ask Nicole to tell Nadine directly how her behavior gets in Nicole's way in making a connection with her.

I (Marianne) am aware that Nicole does enter into the discussion with frequency, yet as a pattern it is often in a reactive manner. She seems to take issue with several members and tends to focus more on what they are doing rather than identifying personal issues that she would be willing to explore. At some time I would want to point out to Nicole that while she is willing to give feedback and her reactions to others, I do not have a clear sense of what she wants to accomplish for herself in the group.

Conflict is a reality in many groups, yet conflict typically is a source of anxiety for group leaders. When conflict occurs, there is a chance for members to encounter one another on an honest level. The manner in which conflict is dealt with will determine whether a group gets stuck or whether interactions among members deepen. The expression of conflict often characterizes the initial and transition stages of a group. This can be viewed as a way for members to create safety and trust in a group. As difficult and challenging as it may be for group leaders to address conflict, they cannot afford to avoid dealing with conflict. Members are not likely to take risks and to allow themselves to be vulnerable if they do not sense safety with the other members and the leaders. If conflict is explored, the chances are increased that members will do significant personal work.

When conflict occurs in this group, observe how members are interacting with one another before intervening. The timing of interventions is crucial here. After getting a sense of how conflict is unfolding, it is a good idea for leaders to explore members' observations about the conflict. Leaders have the task of assisting members in dealing directly and respectfully with their reactions to others. Leaders need to be vigilant in getting members to focus on themselves and express how they are being affected by what is occurring in the group rather than attributing motives to the behavior of others. An important leadership skill is blocking members when they begin attacking each other, and redirecting them to focus on themselves. Leaders cannot prevent unkindness on the part of certain members, but they do need to take action to minimize the detrimental effects that may result from a conflict.

I FEEL WEAK WHEN I SHOW FEELINGS

VIEW VIDEO SECTION 14: I FEEL WEAK WHEN I SHOW FEELINGS

Narration

As the group continues, other members have issues with each other. The diversity and life experiences of group members can have a profound effect on how members view and interact with each other.

Key Points in the Group Session

Maria has a reaction to Galo not listening to her. The focus then shifts to Galo, who very quickly says it is fine by him if Maria is not going to listen to him. Jerry confronts Galo by asking him if it is really fine that others in this group don't listen to him. Galo admits that his parents did not listen to him, and he did not listen to them. Hesitantly, Galo admits that he wants to be listened to, yet he is concerned that if he asks for this he is being weak.

Marianne gives Galo feedback that several members are saying that they want to hear more from him. Marianne asks Galo if he would be willing to check with other members about how they are affected by his quietness. Galo says that it would be scary for him to do so. However, he indicates that it would be less scary for him to talk about how he felt that he never had a voice at home. He adds, "I felt that my opinion was never respected. Showing feelings and emotions was a sign of weakness."

Jerry continues working with Galo by asking him, "Who in your life told you that it was a sign of weakness to show feelings and emotions?" Galo replies that the men in his family said expressing feelings was a sign of weakness.

Maria tells Galo that she respects him for being willing to talk and that she does not see this as a sign of weakness. Maria also tells him that she perceives him as a man by saying, "You are a true man! You are a man!"

Your Reflections and Responses

1. If you were working with Galo, how might you challenge him to take the steps necessary to get what he says he wants? How would Galo's cultural background lead you to modify, if at all, your interventions with him?

_____

_____

_____

2. For each of Galo's statements that follow, think of a brief response you might make as a group leader.

   a. "I never had a voice at home."

   _____

   _____

   _____

   b. "I grew up believing it was a sign of weakness to have and express feelings."

   _____

   _____

   _____

   c. "In my life, people don't seem to listen to me."

   _____

   _____

   _____

   d. "I didn't get my time in this session."

   _____

   _____

   _____

   e. "I want you leaders to call on me."

   _____

   _____

   _____

3. Maria spontaneously gives Galo feedback when she tells him that she views him as a man. Would you ask other members to give him feedback? Why or why not?

   _____

   _____

   _____

Group Leaders' Reflections

I (Jerry) give Galo feedback regarding how it is for me to hear him when he speaks out. It is sad that he has believed the voices that told him he was weak and he didn't have anything of value to say. I want to support Galo in continuing the strides he is making in letting his voice be heard. I like hearing from him when he is challenging those voices. Galo projects his feelings about not being listened to by his family onto the group. He is quick to conclude that the people in the group are just like his family. Possible future work with Galo could involve assisting him in gaining a better perspective on how he carries his belief system into the group. He will then be in a better position to dispute the notion that he is not worthy of having others listen to him.

As Jerry is working with Galo, I (Marianne) am aware that Jerry may be having countertransference reactions with Galo. Like Galo, Jerry often was not listened to by his family. As a coleader, my main concern is that Jerry's possible countertransference does not interfere with Galo's self-exploration or the direction Galo takes in the group. It is important that whatever Jerry suggests to Galo is for Galo's sake, rather than for Jerry's sake.

"What might I (Marianne) do if I believed my coleader was experiencing countertransference, but was not aware of it?" If this were operating with Jerry, I would certainly call my observations to his attention when we meet to process the group and reflect on our work as leaders. After I had an opportunity to discuss Jerry's reactions in the group with him, we might reveal the essence of our discussion if we both thought doing so would be appropriate and would be useful to the group. We do not want any potential countertransference reactions on our part to interfere with any group member's work.

CHECKING OUT: WHAT IS EACH OF YOU TAKING FROM THIS SESSION?

VIEW VIDEO SECTION 15: CHECKING OUT: WHAT IS EACH OF YOU TAKING FROM THIS SESSION?

Narration

As this group session comes to an end, the group leaders use this opportunity to reiterate what was learned and to bring closure. Both Marianne and Jerry bring closure to this group session. The coleaders share some of their observations and ask members to reflect on their experience during the session.

Key Points in the Group Session

Jerry discusses the importance of members talking about what they have learned so far, and what issues they want to bring to the next session. Marianne asks members to notice any shift in thinking they may have experienced over the course of the meetings and what they have learned about conflict.

Your Reflections and Responses

1. If you were leading this group, what kind of observations would you want to make pertaining to this session thus far?

_____

_____

_____

2. What are your thoughts about the level of trust in the group as this session is ending? Specifically, how was this trust facilitated by the leaders and the members? What would you do to help the group continue to build trust?

_____

_____

_____

Group Leaders' Reflections

Just as the checking-in process is helpful in beginning a session, the checking-out process is vital to getting a sense of what the session meant to members. We would like to hear something brief from each member regarding what they are taking away from a given meeting.

I (Jerry) am likely to say to this group, "I hope you begin to see the importance of talking. If you keep your feelings and thoughts pertaining to what is happening in the group to yourself, we won't move forward. I hope each of you will say something about what you are experiencing in the group today and what you want to pursue in the next session."

I (Marianne) would like members to verbalize any shifts they are noticing, especially anything they are learning about conflict. I am apt to ask members to be specific about what it was like for them at the beginning of the session and what they are experiencing at this moment as the session is ending. Some questions I often ask as a way to facilitate closure on each member's part are: "What changes did you make? How did you make these changes? How can you implement this knowledge in your life?"

VIEW VIDEO SECTION COMMENTARY

Key Points in the Commentary

- Look at the reluctance and defensiveness within a group and ask what the behavior is saying.

- What is happening makes sense! Strive to understand the underlying meanings of the behavior of members in the group.

- It may be uncomfortable for the leader, but by not dealing with the defensive behavior, a group does not move ahead.

- Talk about the conflict. It is important to teach members to express their feelings and thoughts about a conflict.

- It is essential for leaders to intervene when members insult each other.

- It is essential to keep members talking during times of conflict to uncover their underlying concerns.

- Members may also begin to recognize their potential transference reactions to one another.

- Members' reactions to one another in group often provide useful information about their life outside the group.

- Ask members what they are experiencing in the group, and explore how they are affected by what is going on.

- Do not give up easily or quickly. Stay with members who are struggling in a group.

- Be watchful of your own countertransference issues as the leader.

- Reframe resistance, and do not assign labels to group members.

IN-CLASS EXERCISE: QUESTIONS FOR SMALL GROUP DISCUSSION AND REFLECTING TEAMS

Form reflecting teams in small groups within your class. This can be done as an entire class activity if the group is small enough. Share your observations and reactions, and remember to avoid judging, diagnosing, and interpreting. In your small group, focus on what you heard and saw during the interactions that stood out for you.

What are some salient moments of the program thus far? Share your thoughts, feelings, and reactions to what you are seeing unfold in the group and reflect on your experience of observing the various vignettes. Pay particular attention to how you are personally affected by the members and the leaders and how that might influence the way you would lead this group.

1. What are your reactions to what the coleaders are doing and what you are learning from this?

2. What would it be like for you to facilitate this group?

3. What would it be like for you to be a participant in this group?

4. What would you most want to teach members about the consequences of not dealing with conflict when it arises in the group?

5. How well do you deal with conflict in your personal life? How ready are you as a group leader to deal with conflict in a group you are leading?

6. How would you work with silence in a group? Would you allow a silence to continue, or would you intervene immediately?

Part III: Challenges of Addressing Diversity Issues

In this segment of the program, we address how diversity can affect the group process. Unless members deal with how they perceive their differences, they are not likely to engage in significant personal or interpersonal work.

WHAT DOES MY CULTURE HAVE TO DO WITH MY IDENTITY?

VIEW VIDEO SECTION INTRODUCTION AND VIDEO 16: WHAT DOES MY CULTURE HAVE TO DO WITH MY IDENTITY?

Narration

Jerry opens the session and talks about how some members had trouble because they felt "different." Members are encouraged to talk about how their differences affect their involvement in the group.

Key Points in the Group Session

Joel begins with, "I have a struggle of how I fit in my life and in this group. I feel I don't have an identity. Should I be a Mexican, a Mexican American, or an American? It's just hard for me to fit in this group and in life. I am often called a coconut, a sellout."

Vivian enters in by saying that she can relate with Joel. She asks how she can keep her own culture while still living in a white society.

Joel comments that he was able to relate to Galo in speaking Spanish and finding comfort with him in this.

Your Reflections and Responses

1. What are some questions you are likely to ask Joel to get a better sense of what he means when he says that he does not have an identity?

_____

_____

_____

2. How would you facilitate work with Joel who says that he wants to explore his cultural identity?

_____

_____

_____

3. What are some possible ways to link Joel's work with that of other members?

_____

_____

_____

4. Vivian struggles to fit in with Vietnamese culture and her American culture. In what ways might you assist her in exploring her concern?

_____

_____

_____

Group Leaders' Reflections

Joel is struggling with his cultural identity. I (Jerry) want to encourage him to talk more about this struggle and how that affects him in his everyday life. Later, when Joel expresses his difficulties of knowing how he fits into the group and in society, my (Jerry) inclination is to invite him to expand on this. He takes an important step in saying what he does. I am struck by Joel's statement, "It's just hard for me to fit in this group and in life."

A useful point of departure could be asking Joel to say more about his difficulties in fitting in this group. Here is how I (Jerry) envision this work might proceed. I ask Joel to address different group members and let each of them know about his difficulties in relating to them. As a result of Joel talking directly to each member, we get a better sense of how he experiences this inability to fit into this group. If he so desires, Joel can let certain members know how he would like to better relate to them. After he completes the go-around, members can be invited to respond to him. Some questions to facilitate this feedback are: "How were you affected by what Joel said? Do any of you relate to Joel's struggle of fitting in, either in the group or in your life?"

At one point in the session Joel comments that he is able to relate to Galo in speaking Spanish and feeling comfortable with him. I (Marianne) suggest that Joel talk directly to Galo about this connection as a way to deepen the work. This would be a good place to facilitate a continued dialogue between Joel and Galo about their connection due to having a common language. As much as possible, I want to link members' concerns so that several group members can work together on similar personal concerns.

Vivian joins in by identifying with Joel regarding her concern about her cultural identity. She is struggling with being a person living in two cultures. A useful intervention is to invite Vivian to talk to Joel about her struggles and for Joel to talk with Vivian about his concerns. As a result of their dialogue, we will get a clearer understanding of how Vivian experiences this concern, how this causes her problems, and what she would like to resolve. As with Joel, members can be asked to respond to Vivian regarding ways they experience her and are able to relate to her. We are striving to do more than merely work with either member individually. Instead, we are thinking of ways to get several members involved by interacting with each other. By linking members who have similar themes, and asking others to react to them, significant steps are taken in creating trust and cohesion.

In working with several bicultural individuals in this group, I (Marianne) need to monitor my own potential countertransference. I have experienced the difficulties of trying to fit into two cultures. My life experiences, which could result in countertransference, can either be an asset or a liability. If I become emotionally overwhelmed as a reaction to listening to others, this could render me ineffective. At the same time, my experiences and feelings can be a real asset in facilitating the work of bicultural members.

I FEEL DIFFERENT FROM OTHERS IN HERE

VIEW VIDEO SECTION 17: I FEEL DIFFERENT FROM OTHERS IN HERE

Narration

Exploring feelings of being different promotes a better understanding for one another.

Key Points in the Group Session

Galo talks to coleaders about his concern of being understood by white people. He asks, "How are you going to understand me because you have not experienced what I have? I don't think you can help me."

Marianne enters in by letting members know that it is impossible for her to know everything about all members' backgrounds.

Galo says that he had a lot of negative experiences with white people while he was growing up.

Jerry asks Galo if he has had negative experiences in this group so far. Although Galo says no, he adds that it is hard for him to get past some of the negative experiences he has had in society. Galo says that it is hard for him to connect in the group because of his belief that all white people have great lives in that they have the money and the power. He says, "That is why it is hard for me to relate with the white people who are in here."

Your Reflections and Responses

1. What might you say to Galo when he tells you that he doubts you can help him because you have not experienced what he has and that you can't understand him?

_____

_____

_____

2. How might your ability to identify with Galo be a help or a hindrance in working with him?

_____

_____

_____

Group Leaders' Reflections

I (Jerry) want to encourage Galo to let me know if he has had or is having any difficulty in relating with me. I think the immediacy of our relationship is an important focus of work that could lead to increased safety. Unless Galo can express his doubts and reservations about me being helpful to him, it is unlikely that he will trust me enough to make himself vulnerable with me by engaging in meaningful personal exploration. However, I also need to be sensitive to a possible cultural injunction against challenging authority, as well as his hesitation to ask for time in the group. In the subsequent session, if Galo does not actively participate, I will check in with him periodically to inquire about what he is experiencing in the group.

I (Jerry) also need to assist him in creating trusting attitudes toward other members. One idea is to ask Galo to bring into the group his concern about not relating to white people. Rather than simply having Galo talk about not relating to white people outside the group, he can be asked to say something to each white person in this group. Beginning with the here and now is a significant bridge to exploring out-of-group concerns, such as feeling discriminated against. By bringing his personal issue into the group, it is possible to get a better sense of what he means by "not relating."

I (Marianne) want the group members to know how difficult it is to know the subtleties of everyone's culture and background. Although it may be a large order to know a great deal about the cultural background of all the members of a group, we can take steps to increase our knowledge of the members' cultural background. When I am leading a diverse group such as this one, I strive to be sensitive in my interventions by checking with them about how helpful certain interventions are. If I make an intervention that does not seem to be going anywhere, or seems to result in confusion on the member's part, I will avoid pressing forward with my agenda. Instead, I will inquire about the possible difficulties regarding what I have asked the member to do.

SOMETIMES I WANT TO EXCLUDE OTHERS
VIEW VIDEO SECTION 18: SOMETIMES I WANT TO EXCLUDE OTHERS

Narration

Nicole feels excluded by Galo when he speaks Spanish with other group members during a break. Both Galo and Joel admit that sometimes their intention is to exclude others.

Key Points in the Group Session

The group leaders allow this discussion to develop without interrupting. Rather than directly addressing the conflict at this point, Marianne asks how this may be affecting others who are bilingual, and Maria responds.

Your Reflections and Responses

1. Do you see any potential alliances shaping up in this group? If so, what are they?

_____

_____

_____

2. What would you say to Galo and Joel when they say that their intention is to exclude others?

_____

_____

_____

3. What would you want to say to Nicole about her feelings of exclusion?

_____

_____

_____

Group Leaders' Reflections

In this session both Galo and Joel admit that they want to exclude others at times. Speaking Spanish was a way they had of forming a bond with each other, which could result in a form of subgrouping. In this scenario, Nicole felt excluded when Joel and Galo spoke Spanish during the break. They admitted that their intention was to exclude others. This is an example of an issue of inclusion and exclusion that needs to be addressed more fully in this group.

Not all subgroupings are problematic. When members meet outside of group sessions, group cohesion might even be increased. Members can extend what they are learning in their group to the informal gatherings. However, forming alliances (subgrouping) can be divisive if members form cliques outside of the group and discuss matters that they are not willing to bring into the whole group. When members form cliques and engage in private dialogues, especially in talking about their reactions pertaining to the group, this separates both these members and others from them and interferes with developing cohesion and trust. Some members are bound to have an affinity toward certain other members, but this could be useful material to make explicit within the group. As group leaders, we see one of our tasks as monitoring possible alliances between members to determine the kind of impact they may have on the whole group.

I STRUGGLE WITH LANGUAGE

VIEW VIDEO SECTION 19: I STRUGGLE WITH LANGUAGE

Narration

As a way to include others in the discussion about language, Marianne asks group members, "How does that fit for others who are bilingual?"

Key Points in the Group Session

Maria says that when she talks about feelings she has to talk in Spanish. When she is in gatherings where most people are speaking English, if there is one person who speaks Spanish, she feels a need to connect with this individual. Maria says that she needs to do this to be who she is. Maria expresses a range of concerns over her differences. Although she is white on the outside, when she speaks English her accent identifies her as being different. As a woman living in the United States, Maria experiences difficulties in being herself. She has concerns about being bilingual, about her accent, and others' reactions to that. She feels embarrassed and stupid. Maria adds that there are layers of experiences that she must address in defending herself as a woman in this country, as a Mexican and as a bilingual and bicultural individual.

Your Reflections and Responses

1. Maria has concerns about being different and feeling stupid because she does not always use the correct English words to express herself. What ideas do you have for assisting Maria in furthering her work?

_____

_____

_____

2. Are you inclined to bring other members into Maria's work? If so, with what purpose? If not, why not?

_____

_____

_____

Group Leaders' Reflections

Group members may have concerns over a multiplicity of differences they experience, both in society and in the group. A few of these differences pertain to age, gender, race, culture, socioeconomic and educational background, and language. A group context provides an ideal setting for members to explore ways they feel different from others in the group and how these differences influence their participation. When members bring up concerns over their differences, it is essential that we pay careful attention to this and invite members to talk further about their concerns as they play out in the context of the group.

I (Marianne) can understand Maria's struggles over her cultural identity and her accent. I want Maria to know that I feel empathy toward her feelings about her accent and being bilingual. In addition, I want to offer her an opportunity work through these feelings. I will encourage her to express herself in the group and not let her fear of being misunderstood stop her. Maria takes on full responsibility for being understood. She could share some of this responsibility with others by requesting: "If you don't understand me, would you let me know?" Doing this frees participants from being embarrassed over their difficulty understanding Maria. Attending to this issue is likely to result in Maria becoming a more active participant.

I RESENT BEING STEREOTYPED

VIEW VIDEO SECTION 20: I RESENT BEING STEREOTYPED

Narration

Group members continue sharing concerns about fitting in.

Key Points in the Group Session

George is having a reaction to the discussion about cultural identity and feels an urgency to jump in and express himself. George feels "put in a box" because he is white. He talks about having struggles similar to those expressed by Galo, Joel, and Maria. He feels that they are not understanding him. He particularly reacts to the comment "because you're white," saying how it stung to hear that.

Marianne asks group members to respond to what they hear George saying. Joel indicates that George is privileged because he is a white male.

After Joel's comment to George about his being privileged because of his white skin, George begins by defending himself. Marianne intervenes with, "Can you hear that? Can you hear that even though you have had many diverse experiences, you are still privileged in this society because of being a white male?" George continues arguing against the notion of his privileged status.

Your Reflections and Responses

1. What stands out most for you regarding what George said about his feeling of being stereotyped as a white male? How might your own gender and cultural identity affect the way in which you react to him, and how you might engage him therapeutically?

_____

_____

_____

2. How are you likely to work with George's statement that he feels "put into a box"? What might you most want to say to him?

_____

_____

_____

3. As Joel was talking, Maria was nodding her head. Would you invite her to speak to Joel? Why or why not?

_____

_____

_____

Group Leaders' Reflections

Stereotyping exists in society, and members are apt to bring their stereotypes into the group and project them onto members and situations that occur within the group. Likewise, racial tension does not simply exist in society at large; members also bring these attitudes and tensions into the group. Groups are not likely to become cohesive or functional if underlying biases, stereotypes, and prejudices are not identified and dealt with effectively.

When I (Marianne) intervene with George by asking him if he can hear what Joel is telling him, I am hoping that George can take in Joel's feedback rather than discounting it. I am aware of how important it is for members to deal with the underlying issues of being stereotyped. Unless members deal with the conflicts that emerge during this discussion, they are not likely to create a climate of trust. This work is a crucial transition that enables them to progress in sharing deeper and more personal aspects of themselves, which characterizes the cohesiveness of a working stage of a group.

WE ARE ALIKE AND WE ARE DIFFERENT

VIEW VIDEO SECTION 21: WE ARE ALIKE AND WE ARE DIFFERENT

Narration

As a result of talking about their differences, some common themes arise.

Key Points in the Group Session

Marianne and Jerry talk about commonalities and differences. Jerry sums up, "So I am hearing a lot of commonalities amongst our differences, which I think can bridge the gap in this particular group."

Nicole returns to her feelings about Galo's statement that when he was speaking with Joel in Spanish he intended to exclude her. Marianne intervenes with a suggestion that Nicole listen without becoming defensive and personalizing what she hears.

Marianne talks about how to communicate feelings of difference and how people often personalize the matter when others speak in their first language.

Jerry makes a connection with Galo in acknowledging and appreciating that Galo has not written him off.

Your Reflections and Responses

1. Would you be inclined to focus on how members feel different from one another or on what they have in common with each other? Explain.

_____

_____

_____

2. What are some common themes that you see emerging in this group?

_____

_____

_____

3. If Galo gave you indications that he is writing you off as a group leader, how would you proceed?

_____

_____

_____

Group Leaders' Reflections

We operate on the assumption that common themes can unite this diverse group and that some universal human dimensions can help us to bridge the gap between our differences. As members talk about their own experiences, especially about feeling different, we are struck by the common themes that seem to arise. A few of these themes include not wanting to be judged, wanting to be heard and understood, and wanting to belong.

The subject of speaking in one's primary language comes up again, with some members being concerned about excluding others or being excluded. I (Marianne) take this opportunity to do a bit of teaching regarding how to avoid personalizing the issue when people speak in a language other than English. When I speak German, some people think I am being rude, insensitive, and excluding people. Yet this is the farthest thing from my mind. For me, speaking German simply means a better connection with another German-speaking person. When Nicole reacts to this matter by personalizing it and becoming defensive, my intent is to understand her and to give her an opportunity to express her feelings about being excluded. At the same time, my hope is that Nicole will learn how to listen to what is being communicated to her without getting defensive.

I EXPRESS MYSELF BETTER IN MY NATIVE LANGUAGE
VIEW VIDEO SECTION 22: I EXPRESS MYSELF BETTER IN MY NATIVE LANGUAGE

Narration
With diversity come the variables of language and of ways of self-expression.

Key Points in the Group Session
Maria is frustrated when she doesn't know how to express her feelings in English. She feels that Nicole is the only person who is interested in understanding her culture.

Jerry suggests to Maria that she might consider using Spanish at times when doing so would help her convey her inner experience to others in this group. Maria admits that she has not considered this, but expresses an openness to the suggestion.

Jerry now asks if Maria would be willing to say something to each person in Spanish. "Maybe you can make the rounds and say one thing in Spanish to each person from your heart that you have wanted to say, but you have held back. How about one line to each person in here?"

Marianne adds to the instructions to Maria in making the rounds, "Say especially the things that you have not said because it is hard to express in English." Maria then makes the rounds in a very emotional and fluid manner, giving the appearance that she has no difficulty in communicating her deep feelings.

Marianne says after Maria makes the rounds, "You see the irony of it all that when someone speaks another language that people won't understand them." Marianne shares her observations of others in the group; although many did not understand Maria's words, they certainly understood her message. Marianne explains what occurred with Maria and how powerful it can be to speak in one's primary language.

Jerry states to the group that he noticed that many people had reactions as Maria was working, and he encourages members to share these reactions.

Vivian admires the work Maria did because of the difficulty Vivian has expressing herself in Vietnamese.

Toni shares with Maria that even though she speaks English only, her control is such that she suppresses feelings that may emerge. However, in listening to Maria, Toni reveals that she was emotionally affected and tears came to her eyes. She says, "I had more feelings in a foreign language than I can bring up in English." She adds, "It was a breakthrough for me because I don't see color and I am colorblind, but this was very different."

Joel shares with Maria that although he understood her words he was even more touched by her feelings.

Nicole reveals that even though she felt excluded earlier when Spanish was being spoken, she felt very included as she listened to Maria speaking in Spanish.

Your Reflections and Responses
1. What were your reactions to Maria as you watched this segment of her work? What feelings and thoughts did she evoke in you?

_____

_____

_____

2. What potentials do you see in asking members to sometimes express themselves in their first language? What effects on the group did you notice from having Maria speak in her primary language?

_____

_____

_____

3. How important is it for you to understand what the group member said in his or her own primary language, and why?

_____

_____

_____

Group Leaders' Reflections

Maria asserts that at times it is difficult for her to express herself and her feelings in English. By inviting her to briefly speak in Spanish, the aim is to free her to speak from her heart. Maria expressed herself with clarity through her emotions in such a way that even those who did not understand Spanish could understand and were affected by her messages. As coleaders, we took our clues from Maria that speaking Spanish at this moment might be helpful to her. It certainly is not necessary for Maria to speak exclusively in Spanish, but as an experiment we invite her to say something to each member in her primary language. We want to encourage others in the group to take the latitude of expressing themselves in whatever language will help them to be more fully themselves.

After Maria's direct comments to each person in the group, Jerry made an open-ended comment that he noticed others were having reactions and asked them to share with Maria how they were affected. Notice that this intervention is open-ended and unstructured. Members are free to speak directly to Maria about how they were affected by what she did. Other members were not called upon to speak, but merely invited to share their reactions. Those who spoke Spanish understood Maria, yet they were touched more by her feelings than by the content of what she said. Others who did not understand Maria's spoken words were still affected by her work, and for some, this could have been a catalyst for them to pursue their own work. For example, feelings arose for Toni that she could do more within the group. Maria's work was a turning point for her, but it also increased the cohesion and trust in the group.

I AM COLORBLIND
VIEW VIDEO SECTION 23: I AM COLORBLIND

Narration

When group members state that they do not notice racial and cultural differences, this elicits strong reactions from others.

Key Points in the Group Session

Toni reveals that when she meets a person she does not see color and refers to herself as "colorblind." Marianne asks about Toni's expression of "colorblindness," and the group reacts to this issue.

Toni clarifies what she means by being colorblind. Galo has strong reactions to what she is saying and lets her know that he disagrees that all people are treated as equal. He does want Toni to know that he is different, that he a different color, and that he has a different culture and set of beliefs.

Toni attempts to convince Galo that it does not matter that he is of a different color and a different cultural background. Galo disagrees, and he tells her what is most important that she understands about him.

As Toni and Galo continue interacting, they come to a better understanding of how they perceive their cultural differences and how they want to be viewed.

Although Galo and Toni seem to arrive at a point of better understanding, Marianne intervenes wondering if the issue of being colorblind is being fully addressed because Toni persists in not seeing Galo's brown skin.

Galo challenges Toni's assumptions that because he has brown skin he is from Mexico. He says, "It is important that you ask where I am from, because I am not Mexican. I was born in the United States and my parents are from Central and South America."

Joel brings himself in by saying to Toni, "I have a problem with you saying that you are colorblind and that everybody is the same. I feel that you are trying to deny that stereotypes and discrimination exist." Marianne asks Joel, "How do you want Toni to see you?" Joel says that he wants her to know that people of color and various ethnic backgrounds do struggle in this society.

Marianne reflects and summarizes what Galo and Joel may want Toni to hear. She adds, "If you deny my color, you deny a part of who I am."

Your Reflections and Responses

1. Toni's comment about not noticing a member's color stirs up reactions from some of the members. When you heard Toni state that she is colorblind, what reactions did this evoke in you?

_____

_____

_____

_____

2. How might you work with reactions that members have about hearing Toni's statement?

_____

_____

_____

3. What is your reaction to Marianne's comment, "If you deny my color, you deny who I am"?

_____

_____

_____

_____

Group Leaders' Reflections

At an earlier point in the group, I (Marianne) reacted to Toni saying she was "colorblind." I chose not to pursue her remark at that moment because several other things were going on and I did not want to interrupt the process. However, I filed away my observations and brought them up a short time later. I wondered out loud if anyone else had reactions to Toni's comment. Indeed, several members did, and it helped the group to clarify some misunderstandings about Toni's reference to not seeing color. At that moment, I was concerned that Toni's remark possibly did not set well with some group members. I initiated checking this out by asking if members had reactions to her remark about colorblindness. By providing an opportunity for others to say what may be on their mind, my aim is to prevent a hidden agenda from developing as well as not letting a lot of unchecked assumptions and misunderstandings go unnoticed.

I KNOW LITTLE ABOUT MY CULTURE
VIEW VIDEO SECTION 24: I KNOW LITTLE ABOUT MY CULTURE

Narration

The concern about judgments and stereotypes continues to be a theme in the group. Marianne says more on stereotypes, and she cautions about problems in pushing members to disclose too quickly. She encourages members to decide for themselves what they will disclose, as well as when and how much to disclose. Marianne also addresses the issue that some members' personal disclosures will further stereotype their culture.

Key Points in the Group Session

Nadine enters into the discussion. She reports that the reason she came to the group is the reason she feels uncomfortable in the group. Nadine says that she doesn't fit with any cultural group. She identifies herself as partly Black and mostly Native American, yet adds that she knows very little about her cultural background.

Marianne reflects Nadine's earlier statement about her goals in the group, which involve getting increased clarity of who she is. Marianne invites Nadine to pursue further work in getting this clarity as the sessions unfold.

Marianne comments to both Nadine and Vivian about protecting their culture and their hesitation in deciding what to say because of not wanting to feed a stereotype.

Vivian shares that she is trying to balance herself between two cultures. She is learning that she is not alone in her struggle and relates to Nadine.

Nadine reports that she is the first person in her family to go to college. She says, "I get comments and looks that imply by being Black I come from an ignorant bunch of people."

Joel relates to Nadine, saying that he is hesitant to share with people that he is a graduate student because not many Latinos go to graduate school or become professionals. Joel points to a commonality he feels with Nadine—he feels somewhat lost, by himself, and doesn't know his cultural identity. Like Nadine, Joel finds that he needs to challenge many stereotypes pertaining to his culture.

Your Reflections and Responses

1. How might Nadine's confusion about her culture influence her participation in the group?

_____

_____

_____

2. How would you respond to a member who states, "There is really nobody in this group that I can identify with"?

_____

_____

_____

3. How can you respect members' cultural values about not sharing private and personal information regarding their family, and at the same time assist them in disclosing enough to become participants in the group?

_____

_____

_____

4. If you are guilty of having certain stereotypes that are being explored in this session, as a leader, would you disclose this? Why or why not?

_____

_____

_____

Group Leaders' Reflections

This segment of the program highlights the importance of working with ways in which members' diversity affects their participation in the group. I (Marianne) am aware that I do not want to challenge members to do what is culturally inappropriate for them, such as suggesting that they talk about their family if they made it clear that this is not something they want to do. With help from the leaders they can pursue any issues they have with their family or culture in a way that minimizes feelings of disloyalty and betrayal. If they do make disclosures about their family or culture, I want to be open in exploring any possible regrets they may have about doing so. It may also be a good idea to again address matters of confidentiality. Sometimes members worry about the leader's or members' perceptions about their entire culture based on what they have revealed. We communicate to such members that we fully realize that we are only finding out one aspect of their family or culture and that we don't make judgments based on what they have shared. Unless we attend to members' worries that others will judge their culture, members are not likely to fully participate in a meaningful way.

I WANT MORE ANSWERS FROM YOU LEADERS
VIEW VIDEO SECTION 25: I WANT MORE ANSWERS FROM YOU LEADERS

Narration

It is not uncommon for group members to seek answers from the leader because they perceive the leader as the expert. As the session moves forward, the leaders again bring up the relevance of addressing diversity matters.

Key Points in the Group Session

Vivian states, "And I kind of feel that I am the only one here who is Asian, and I don't really connect with anyone here either. So, I kind of look to the leaders as my authority figures. The more I sit here the more confused I get. I'm wanting answers from you—clean, clear cut answers, not this in-between stuff, because that is what I am struggling with. What I am here for is for both of you leaders to give me straight answers."

Jerry tells Vivian that he doesn't have clear-cut answers for her. Jerry reflects Vivian's and others' cultural struggle and encourages Vivian to continue talking. Vivian demonstrates some insight that it is up to her, with some guidance from the leaders, to come to terms with the issues she has raised.

Jerry asks Vivian what she needs from each of us so that she can do her work in the group. She replies that she wants to know how others deal with similar life issues, would like to hear feedback, emphasizes the importance of confidentiality, and lets Joel know that her identifying with him has helped her to get a better understanding her life situation.

Jerry asks Nadine how her concerns outside of the group affect her in the group. Nadine shares how she sees some commonalities with others, such as sharing in the same fears and feelings of inadequacies. By listening to the stories of others, she is getting a better sense of herself. She acknowledges that she has been able to open herself up in this group and not feel judged. Earlier Nadine made comments about not fitting into this group, and now she is identifying with several members. A shift has obviously taken place for Nadine, which is illustrated by what she says about being able to connect with others, especially Joel and Maria.

Your Reflections and Responses

1. Is it common for members to want answers from group leaders? What would motivate a member to expect answers from group leaders? How would you respond to such requests?

_____

_____

_____

2. What are your reactions to Jerry's response that he does not have clear-cut answers for Vivian?

_____

_____

_____

3. Were there times in this particular program when you might have been tempted to provide members with answers? If so, with whom?

_____

_____

_____

Group Leaders' Reflections

Vivian experiences difficulty in not getting direct answers to her concerns. She is perceiving both of us as the experts with knowledge and answers to problems. I (Jerry) acknowledge to Vivian that I don't have definitive answers for her. However, I don't want to communicate to her that I am rendered helpless with her. I am likely to ask her what I need to know about her in order for me to help her find the answers she is seeking. What she says will give me significant information that can assist me in working with her. There are many ways that I can assist her in gaining clarity and insights regarding her inner conflicts, if she is willing to continue talking about them. With Vivian, some future work might entail asking her to stay a bit longer with what it is like in her world to be fully Vietnamese and as a Vietnamese how might she react to others in the group. Then she could be what she sees as being fully American and what this would entail. By staying longer with one side, she may get a better sense of any difficulties associated with being one or the other sides. She may realize that she does not have to give up one culture for the other. Much of her work will entail discovering how she would like to operate in her world as a person living with both cultures.

I (Marianne) have had a similar conflict to Vivian's. Being bicultural often evokes feelings of disloyalty. In my own life I have found that if I identity myself as German, I wonder if I am being disloyal to the American part of me. If I acknowledge myself as an American, am I being disloyal to the German part of me? What further complicates this issue is the fact that my family of origin is German, living in Germany. At times I have dealt with fears of letting them down by no longer considering myself fully part of them. Vivian might well be experiencing similar conflicts, but I would not want to impose my experience on her situation. In some way, I may have some of the answers that Vivian is seeking. However, as tempting as it may be, I do not want to describe my answers to her because they are answers for me and not answers for Vivian. I must exert caution in assuming that her situation is indeed similar to mine. I am again reminded of the importance of monitoring countertransference reactions.

COMMENTARY

VIEW THE REMAINDER OF THE VIDEO PROGRAM: "CHALLENGES"

Narration

Again, the Coreys help group members reflect on their group experience together. Marianne asks how the members were affected through their participation in the group.

Key Points in the Commentary

- Get the group to talk about how diversity is helping or hindering them in the group.
- The group members learn respect for differences, and they also see areas of commonality.
- It is important for group members to bring up how they feel different from others.
- Leaders need to identify differences and commonalities in the group and the impact of these factors on what is evolving.
- It is important to get members to talk about their personal problems in everyday life, but also to facilitate a discussion of what is going on with them within the context of the here-and-now group setting. Leaders need to assist members in bringing into the group sessions any concerns, thoughts, and feelings they are having about being in the group.
- Don't make assumptions about an individual based on his or her cultural background. Always check out your assumptions.

- Don't assume you need to know everything about every member's culture, but remain open to learning what may be salient for each of the members.
- Diversity does not need to be a source of division within a group; it can be a unifying factor and can add richness to the group.

CLOSING COMMENTARY

- Group leaders can never anticipate what will happen. It is never possible to have a perfect lesson plan. What is useful is being present with whatever is happening and not having a preconceived agenda.
- Realize what the group member is saying and its importance to that person. Strive to understand the context in which the member's behavior makes sense.
- Expect the unexpected in your group.

IN-CLASS EXERCISE: QUESTIONS FOR SMALL GROUP DISCUSSION AND REFLECTING TEAMS

Now that you have viewed the dealing with diversity material, share your observations and reactions. In your small group, focus on what you heard and saw, what interactions stood out for you, and the most salient moments of this segment on diversity. What members were you most noticing, and why? What observations did you have about the unfolding of the group process? What are you learning about how you might best work with diversity within a group?

Pay particular attention to how you are personally affected by the members and the leaders and how that might influence the way you would lead this group, or how you would participate as a member. Discuss with one another your reactions to what the coleaders are doing and what you are learning from this. In your group, share your reactions about what challenges you would expect to face if you were leading this group.

1. What value do you see when inviting members to talk in their primary language when engaged in a role play?
2. What are your thoughts about leaders needing to be bicultural in order to be effective with bicultural clients?
3. How might you intervene when you observe stereotyping taking place?
4. When members say they have been discriminated against and oppressed, what interventions will you make to prevent this from evolving into an abstract discussion about society at large? How can you facilitate a more personal interaction within the present context of the group?
5. How might you deal with a group member who is insensitive toward others?
6. What, if any, responsibility do you have as a leader when members show evidence of racism, ethnocentricity, prejudices, and stereotypes?

WHERE ARE YOU NOW AND WHERE WILL YOU GO FROM HERE?

As a final exercise, we ask you to reflect on your significant learnings after viewing *Challenges Facing Group Counselors* and to clarify where you want to go from here.

1. If you were leading this group, what kind of specific member behavior do you think would present the greatest challenge to you? Explain.

_____

_____

_____

_____

_____

2. If you had to identify what you consider to be the major challenge you face (or expect to face) in dealing with diversity within a group, what would this be? Explain.

_____

_____

_____

_____

_____

_____

3. What are some important lessons you have learned about dealing with a range of problematic situations that occur within a group?

_____

_____

_____

_____

_____

_____

4. From watching and reflecting on the group, what did you learn most about yourself personally? What did you learn about yourself as a group leader?

_____

_____

_____

_____

_____

_____

5. What are some life experiences, skills, and knowledge you could draw upon in leading this particular group?

_____

_____

_____

_____

_____

_____

6. What are some skills you most need to acquire or refine to more effectively address the challenging situations you observed?

_____

_____

_____

7. What leader skills did you observe that either helped or hindered the group process? What helped or hindered the development of cohesion and trust within the group?

_____

_____

_____

_____

_____

_____

8. What did you learn that you could you could use with populations you are likely to work with in a group setting?

_____

_____

_____

_____

_____

_____

IN-CLASS EXERCISE: QUESTIONS FOR SMALL GROUP DISCUSSION AND REFLECTING TEAMS

Form reflecting teams in small groups within your class. After writing your responses to the questions in Where Are You Now and Where Will You Go From Here? discuss your answers. Focus on what you learned from this program with respect to dealing with difficult group members, addressing diversity issues, working therapeutically with reluctance, and creating a safe environment where members can pursue meaningful work.

Lecturette on Theories and Techniques of Group Counseling

Overview

In the *Groups in Action* video and workbook, this new Part 3 consists of a 1-hour lecture describing the main theoretical approaches to group work. In this lecture, Jerry Corey covers the basic concepts of the four general theories briefly described in a new chapter in *Groups: Process and Practice* (M. Corey, G. Corey, & C. Corey, 2014) titled "Theories and Techniques of Group Counseling" as well as describing an integrative approach.

We have added this overview lecture to the video program to balance out the two working videos in this series. A theory provides you with a structure for designing appropriate interventions and for evaluating the outcomes of the group as a whole and of the individual members. A theory informs the way you operate in facilitating a group. It guides your work with members and defines both your roles and the members' roles in a group. A theory provides a frame of reference for understanding the world of the client, especially when it comes to making an assessment, defining problems, and selecting appropriate techniques in meeting the goals of the members. Your approach should be flexible enough to meet the unique needs of your group members.

It is particularly important that you develop a personal theoretical approach toward the practice of group counseling that is compatible with your personality and leadership style. If you are unable to draw on theory to support your interventions, group members may not achieve the maximum benefit.

Most theories have a variety of techniques for use in group counseling, and some techniques are applicable to more than one theory. The four general categories of theoretical orientations described in this lecture program are:

1. **Psychodynamic approaches**, which explore the individual's past and work toward gaining insight in therapy (psychoanalytic and Adlerian therapy).

2. **Experiential** and **relationship-oriented approaches**, which value feelings and subjective experiencing (existential, person-centered, Gestalt therapy, and psychodrama).

3. **Cognitive behavioral approaches**, which focus on the role of thinking and doing and tend to be action-oriented (behavior therapy, cognitive therapy, cognitive behavior therapy, rational emotive behavior therapy, and reality therapy).

4. **Postmodern approaches**, which stress understanding the subjective world of the client and tapping the existing resources within the individual for change (solution-focused brief therapy, narrative therapy, and feminist therapy).

This categorization of models is somewhat arbitrary. Overlapping concepts and themes make it difficult to neatly compartmentalize these theoretical orientations. In addition to these four general categories, the lecture includes discussion of an **integrative approach**, which borrows and integrates concepts and techniques from a number of different approaches.

The workbook includes the Main Points covered in the lecture and Questions for Reflection and Discussion for each theoretical orientation.

Part I: Introduction

INTRODUCTION
VIEW VIDEO LECTURETTE 1: INTRODUCTION

Main Points

- A theory will guide you as a group counselor in determining what you want to accomplish, the best methods for getting there, and how to evaluate what you have accomplished.

- It is like flying a plane with a flight plan in place—it informs you of where you are going, the best route for getting there, and how to know when you have reached your destination.

- The major approaches to group counseling addressed in this program are the psychodynamic approaches, experiential and relationship-oriented approaches, cognitive behavioral approaches, and postmodern approaches.

- An integrative approach, which looks at clients from a thinking, feeling, and doing (behavior) perspective and attempts to address all three aspects of the person, is also described.

Questions for Reflection and Discussion

1. Do you see yourself as a group counselor subscribing to a singular approach (such as cognitive behavioral) or a more integrative approach that taps into a variety of theories? Do you think you have adequate knowledge of the various approaches to make this decision at this point?

---

2. How do think your life experiences and your personality style influence your choice of a group approach to counseling?

---

3. Which of the various approaches interests you most at this point in your training? Describe how it is relevant for you.

---

4. Which approach would you most like to learn more about, and what specifically would you like to learn?

Part II: Lecturettes on Theoretical Approaches

PSYCHODYNAMIC APPROACHES

VIEW VIDEO LECTURETTE 2: THE PSYCHODYNAMIC APPROACHES

Main Points

- Psychodynamic approaches to group counseling focus on the client's past and how that past helps clients understand what they are doing in the present.

- Transference and countertransference are major concepts in this approach.

- Groups offer many opportunities for the exploration of transference reactions that have roots in prior relationships. The group constellation lends itself to multiple transferences, which provides material that can be used to reenact past unfinished events. A basic tenet of psychodynamic therapy groups is the idea that group members, through their interactions within the group, re-create their social situation. In this way, that the group becomes a microcosm of members' everyday lives.

- Countertransference issues are common occurrences for group leaders. The key is to be aware of those issues, understand how they affect your group leadership skills, and get help to work on those reactions outside the group.

- The Adlerian perspective is a psychodynamic approach that focuses on the common good of a group. The group leader strives to enhance group interaction by building a sense of community through group process.

- The Adlerian approach focuses on how the client is functioning today by looking at the family of origin and by seeing the group as a microcosm of how one is in one's family and in society.

Questions for Reflection and Discussion

1. How much of a psychodynamic focus did the Coreys use in their work with the groups in Parts 1 and 2 of the *Groups in Action: Evolution and Challenges* video? Were there particular group members for whom a psychodynamic approach made the most sense?

2. What countertransference issues might arise in your work with groups? For which clients in the video would you have been most likely to have a countertransference reaction? What would you have done about that reaction? Would you discuss your reaction with the group?

3. Which of the groups' members would you be most effective working with? Which would you feel least effective working with? Explain.

4. How does your past help you understand who you are currently? How important do you think it is to have a good understanding of your past and how it affects your functioning today? Is it more important for you to focus on the present than to be concerned about the past and its possible influence? What value do you place on the future orientation?

Main Points

- These approaches are referred to as experiential because of the assumption that the best way to learn is by experiencing rather than by "talking about" an issue. In addition, the focus on emotion is the route to the change process.

- These approaches are also referred to as relationship-oriented because the methods focus on the relationships among group members and among the leader and the group members as the way to bring about insight and change.

- Techniques are always secondary to understanding the world of the group member.

- The main task of the group leader is to create a climate of safety and trust within the group that will allow and encourage members to be who they really are.

- Common denominators of this group approach include focusing on emotion, the counselor's ability to be fully present in the group, and the group leader's self-disclosure and sharing what one is experiencing in the group.

- Existential approaches address anxiety, freedom, choice, and responsibility.

- Person-centered approaches take their lead from the group members. The group leader is present, authentic, accepting, and empathic—and attends to what is happening in the group from moment to moment.

- Gestalt approaches emphasize awareness and direct experiencing to focus on the here and now and the ways in which members are relating to one another.

Questions for Reflection and Discussion

1. How does your personal style in leading a group affect the group's functioning? In what ways does it enhance or hinder group functioning and progress?

_____

_____

_____

2. Could you see yourself using a Gestalt technique like the one used with Casey in which she talked with her Mom in her native language? Is that kind of approach consistent with your style and personality?

_____

_____

_____

3. What place do experiential approaches have in your role as a group leader? What do you need to learn to be able to use these approaches effectively?

_____

_____

_____

4. Are you able to remain present when there is an emotional focus in the group? Would you be able to be present in the group and yet remain objective in a way that would allow you to effectively facilitate the group process?

_____

_____

_____

VIEW VIDEO LECTURETTE 4: THE COGNITIVE BEHAVIORAL APPROACHES

Main Points

- Cognitive behavioral approaches include behavior therapy, cognitive behavioral therapy, cognitive therapy, rational emotive behavior therapy, and reality therapy, to name a few.
- Of all the therapeutic approaches utilized today, the cognitive behavioral ones are the most common.
- These therapeutic approaches emphasize collaboration, planning, accountability through research for best methods, structure, and a focus on specific themes and problems.
- Cognitive behavioral approaches view psychological distress as a function of faulty thinking, and therapy is focused on developing more constructive ways of thinking.
- Most cognitive behavioral approaches are psychoeducational; they provide information, teach skills, and value homework as a useful technique.
- In cognitive behavioral approaches awareness of diversity issues and how the various approaches fit with a diverse group are essential.

Questions for Reflection and Discussion

1. What value do you place on the cognitive behavioral approaches when compared with the experiential approaches? Which would you be more comfortable with as a group leader? As a group member? Why?

_____

_____

_____

2. When thinking about the role of emotions, thinking, and behavior in group process, do you believe any one of those factors is more important in bringing about change?

_____

_____

_____

3. Early on in the first group, the Coreys make contracts with each of the group members concerning what each individual would like to accomplish. Do you like the idea of establishing individual goals, or do you think the group should decide what direction to pursue?

_____

_____

_____

4. What irrational beliefs do you have that might affect your work as a group leader? Write down some of those faulty thoughts (for example, "I must be in control in every group situation."), and then write down a more realistic thought for each one.

_____

_____

_____

POSTMODERN APPROACHES
VIEW VIDEO LECTURETTE 5: THE POSTMODERN APPROACHES

Main Points

- Solution-focused brief therapy, narrative therapy, feminist therapy, and multicultural approaches are some of the major postmodern group approaches.

- A common theme in all postmodern approaches is the concept of empowerment of group members, meaning that they are resourceful and have the capacity to change direction in their lives.
- A group is an ideal setting for members to learn how to move from a powerless stance in life to a powerful one.
- Another key notion common among these approaches is that the client is the expert. Group members know best their own situation and solutions for change.
- Social justice has become a focus in group work, particularly for postmodern approaches.
- Techniques commonly utilized in solution-focused brief therapy are the miracle question, the exception question, and the use of homework.
- Feminist approaches ask group members how to create change in the social world in which they live.
- These approaches all respect and attend to diversity issues. A group leader ethically cannot ignore culture and cultural differences among group members.

Questions for Reflection and Discussion

1. Do you agree with the postmodern notion that the client is the expert and that the client has the power to make change? If so, how would you go about creating an atmosphere in group where that can happen?

2. Try out the miracle question for yourself. If you went to sleep tonight and woke up in the morning and your life was exactly the way you would like it to be, what would that look like? What would you be doing? Where would you be? How might you make use of the miracle question in a group setting?

3. How do you think culture and cultural differences affect group functioning? Would your use of group techniques differ depending on the cultural diversity within your group? Explain how you would address these differences.

4. In the *Challenges Facing Group Leaders* video (Part 2), Vivian talks about wanting answers for herself from the group leaders, and she feels their task is to tell her what she should be doing. How would you work with Vivian to help her identify the strengths and resources she owns in becoming more empowered? What are the cultural issues that might influence your work with her?

AN INTEGRATIVE APPROACH

VIEW VIDEO LECTURETTE 6: AN INTEGRATIVE APPROACH

Main Points

- An integrative approach borrows concepts and techniques from a number of different approaches.
- From psychodynamic and experiential and relationship-oriented approaches, you will find ways to focus on relationship issues.

- From the cognitive behavioral approaches, you can use a number of techniques to change faulty thinking and to increase desired behaviors.
- From postmodern approaches, you can find ways to incorporate members' life stories and the concept of their life context.
- Adopting an integrative approach is not simple; you cannot pick and choose various techniques smorgasbord style. Rather you draw upon the various approaches and process them through your own filter so that your approach fits your style and personality, and fits well with the particular group you are leading.
- Adopting an integrative approach takes learning, experience, supervision, and refinement. Over time, as you gain more experience and competence with your approach and your work, your integrative approach will change and evolve.

Questions for Reflection and Discussion

1. At this point in your training or career, are you using an integrative approach in group counseling? What more do you need to learn about an integrative approach?

2. What are the pros and cons of adopting an integrative approach?

3. Can you identify the various aspects of the integrative approach the Coreys were using in their groups? Do you think their approach varied from the first to the second group in the video program?

4. In a perfect world, what knowledge and skills as a group leader would you have? What do you believe it will take for you to get to that place? What might get in the way of your accomplishing that goal? What resources do you have to help you accomplish that goal?

FINAL THOUGHTS

We hope you have enjoyed the *Groups in Action* program and can use the practical information provided in your training or work setting. The program in its entirety provides a first-hand look at how we (Jerry and Marianne Corey) lead two different groups. Our aim has been to encourage you to reflect on ways you can implement your learnings—the techniques and ideas—as a group leader. Becoming a skilled group leader is truly a career-long process of learning about theories and techniques, and how they fit with your personality and your therapeutic style.